DIGITAL KNOWLEDGE MANAGEMENT

in the University Library and Information Centers in Chennai (Madras) an Analytical Study

DIGITAL
KNOWLEDGE MANAGEMENT

in the University Library and Information Centers
in Chennai (Madras) an Analytical Study

Dr.K.SEKAR M.Com., MLIS., M.Phil.,Ph.D.

Librarian i/c
AMET- University, Kanathur

Chennai.600 112

Chennai New Delhi

This edition has been published in india by arrangement with Carson Books, UK

ISBN 9789355284303

MJP Publishers
No. 44, Nallathambi Street,
Triplicane, Chennai 600 005

Printed and bound in India

MJP 1665

Publisher : C. Janarthanan

Acknowledgement

First of all, I would like to thank and praise **The God Almighty** for giving me the spirit and moral strength to complete this study

I express with a deep sense of gratitude and respects to my research supervisor, **Dr. V. KASIRAO**, Principal Documentation Officer & Head, Department of Documentation and Information Science, CSIR-Central Leather Research Institute, Ministry of Science and Technology, Government of India, Adyar, Chennai, for the valuable suggestions, able guidance and sincere help during the course of the investigation and without his direction, constant encouragement, support and expertise, the research work would not have been completed.

I would also like to thank the **Management of AMET University** for providing me excellent Library resources, high speed internet facilities, and valuable online resources and for all academic and administrative support provided for the smooth conduct of the research study.

I am very grateful to **Dr. J. Ramachandran**, Founder - Chancellor, and **Col. Dr. G. Thiruvasagam**, Pro-Chancellor (Academics) AMET University, **Prof. Dr. V. Rajendran,** Vice-Chancellor, **Dr. R. Muthezhilan,** Registrar and **Dr. P.Saravanan** Former Registrar and **Dr. M. Jayaprakashvel**, Co-Ordinator, IQAC for their support and permission to do my research work.

I extend my thanks to **Mrs. A. Sheela Devi**, Librarian, Thanthai Periyar Govt. Institute of Technology, Bagayam, Vellore, **Ms. K. Sandhiya**, Asst. Professor, Dept. of Civil Engineering, Tagore

Engineering College, Vandalur, Chennai, **Er. K. Sathish Kumar, Mr. I.G. Hariharan, Mr. K. Jai Shankar,** staff members of the Department of Documentation and Information Science, CSIR-CLRI for their support and encouragement.

Finally, I would like to express my heartfelt gratitude to one and all who directly or indirectly have lent their hand in executing this work in a successful way.

(K. SEKAR)

Preface

Digital Knowledge Management (DKM) plays a vital role in the present digital knowledge Era. It provides effective, efficient information and knowledge management services to the library user community in time and on demand. Knowledge management represented as a cross-disciplinary domain which can relate to a wide range of disciplines and technologies such as cognitive science, knowledge based management system, Library and information science, Documentation management, Relational and object orientated database and management of information and people. The Digital Knowledge Management as a tool for supporting the creation, achieving and sharing of valued information to facilitate the web based solution to know-how the technologies on Digital /Electronics learning to support the ICT Technologies towards organizational development.

The Information and Communication Technology tools are inevitable for **K**nowledge **A**ccess and **S**haring **I**nformation for **R**esources **A**pproach **O**bjectives (KASIRAO) in the present e-knowledge society. The ICT serves as a tool for efficient Management of Information, that is storage, retrieval, processing communication, diffusing and sharing of knowledge for Socio-Economic and Cultural Development. The impact of Information Communication Technology (ICT) encourages the library user community to search and to retrieve the required information. It also helps the knowledge economy by promoting Digital Knowledge Management and objectively that the application of Information Communication Technology in the University Library and

Information Centers would certainly put on order and bring out a sequence operations in Library and Information Management Environment (LISME) without much of human interventions.

Based on the conceptual analysis view, the research study identifies the State-of-the-Art of the Digital Knowledge Management and ICT applications in the State, Central and Deemed University Libraries in Chennai. The study identifies the factors like lack of finance and training to hinder the promotion of ICT in Libraries and to promote it offers suggestions for effective implementation of ICT application tools for digital knowledge management services in the Library and Information Centers.

(K. SEKAR)

List of Abbreviations

ALA	American Library Association
ASCE	American Society of Civil Engineers
ASME	American Society of Mechanical Engineers
AVR	Audio Visual Resources
BB	Book Bank
BV	Back Volume
CALIBNET	Calcutta Library Network
CAS	Current Awareness Services
CAS	Current Awareness Service
CCTV	Closed Circuit Television
CD –ROM	Compact Disk-Read Only Memory
CD/DVD	Compact Disc/Digital Video disc
CDP	Collection Development Policy
CDROM	Compact Disc Read Only Memory
CERA	Consortium for e-resources in Agricultural
CIO	Chief Information Officers
Cir	Circulation
CISR	Council of Scientific and Industrial Research
CP	Current Periodicals
CU	Central University
DCMS	Digital content management services
DDS	Document Delivery Service
DEB	Digital Environment Barriers
DELNET	Developing Library Network

DKM	Digital Knowledge Management
DKRC	Digital Knowledge Resource Centre
DL	Digital Library
DNB	Digital notice board
DPI	Digital Procurement Image
DRM	Digital rights management
DRS	Digital Reference Service
DRS	Digital repository services
DU	Deemed University
E-B	Electronic Book
E-databases	Electronic databases
EJ	Electronic journals
EL	E-literature search
E-Mail	Electronic Mail
EMRC	Educational and Multimedia Research Center
EN	E-newspaper
EP	Electronic publications
ERNET	Educational Resource Network
ETD	Electronic Thesis and Dissertation
FORSA	Forum for Resource Sharing in Astronomy and
FP	Faculty publication
GSDL	Green Stone Digital Library
HELINET	Health Sciences Library and Information Network
I & A	Indexing and Abstracting
ICT	Information and Communication Technology
IDCs	Information and Documentation Centers
IEEE	Institute of Electrical and Electronic Engineers
IJ	International Journal
IKM	Impact on Knowledge Management

ILL	Inter Library Loan
IM	Information Management
INDEST	Indian National Digital Library in Engineering Sciences
INDONET	Data Network
INFLIBNET	Information and Library Network
IP	Internet Protocol
IT	Information Technology
KASIRAO	Knowledge Access and Sharing Information for Resource Approach Objectives
KBMS	Knowledge based Management Systems
KMPM	Knowledge Management Process Model
KOMS	Knowledge Organization and Management Skills
LAN	Local Area Network
LICs	Library and Information centers
LIME	Library Information Management Environment
LISME	Library and Information management Environment
M. Phil.	Master of Philosophy
MALIBNET	Madras Library Network
MANIBLET	Management of Library Network
MDGS	Millennium Development Goals
MEDLARS	Medical Literature Analysis and Retrieval System
MOOC	Massive Open Online Course
MUDR	Manipal University Digital Repository
NBM	Non Book Material
NCR	National Capital Region
NDL	National Digital Library
NICNET	National Informatics Centre Network
NISSAT	National Information System for Science & Technology

NJ	National Journal
NKN	National Knowledge network
N-LIST	National Library and Information Services Infrastructure for Scholarly Content
NME-ICT	National Mission in Education through ICT
NPTEL	National Programme on Technology Enhanced Learning
NTF	National Task Force
OAR	Open Access Resource
OCR	Optical Characters Recognition
OER	Online Education Resource
OPAC	Online Public Access Catalogue
OPAC	Online Public access catalogue
OSS	Open Source Software
PDF	Portable Document File
PEC	Punjab engineering college
PG	Post Graduate
PMDP	Personnel Management Development Policy
QR	Quick reference
RAM	Random Access Memory
RDF	Resource Description Framework
REF B	Reference Books
RES	Reservation
RFID	Radio Frequency Identification
SDI	Selective Dissemination of Information
SIRNET	Scientific and Industrial Research Network
SLA	Special Library Association

SMS	Short message service
SMS	Short Message Service
SNS	Social Network Services
SNS	Social Networking Site
SOUL	Software for University Library
SPSS	Statistical Package for Social Sciences
SU	State University
SWAYAM	Study Webs of Active-Learning for Young Aspiring Minds
TQM	Total Quality Management
UG	Under Graduate
UGC	Union Grants Commission
UML	Unified Modeling Language
URL	Uniform Resource Locater
VCR	Video Cassette Record
VL	Virtual Library
VMC	Vicarious Management Corporation
WOL	Web Ontology Language

Contents

Table of Contents

List of Figures

Chapter I

INTRODUCTION

1.1 PREAMBLE

Information is all pervasive elements in the contemporary society. Every social trend cause some influence on the future shapes of information services in any information center, whether it is public or academic or special or similar services institutions. On one hand, the information services are reacting to the changing trends and new dimensions in the society and on the other, the services are enhanced through the application of Information Technology (IT), The Information Communication Technology (ICT) offers avenues for easy access to information, crossing the barriers of communication (Kasi Rao 2014).

The Roots ICT can be traced back to the ancient civilization. With the ever-increasing growth in information, the application of information and communication can be seen during the past two decades. This may be due to (i) economic and social needs and (ii) technological innovation.

The recent advancements in ICT have changed the world scenario. This ICT revolution has affected each and every aspect of human society and has opened new opportunities and challenges for all. The developments have also imposed certain responsibilities and challenges on Information management professionals.

The development in Information Communication Technology and their use in India are currently dominating. The application of ICT in different types of libraries in India has gained sufficient momentum and it is of continuing interest to the information professionals in order to provide ICT based services.

The Library and information centers (LICs) play a vital role in educating and empowering citizens through the applications of ICT for Knowledge Access and Sharing Information for Resources Approach Objectives (KASIRAO) in the present digital knowledge based society (Kasi Rao 2013). In view of this, the electronic resources are the prime ingredients and they become a common part of the academic library resources today. Internet and its most useful component, World Wide Web (WWW) has turned into the biggest source of information with the widest coverage of the speedy access. It is the most powerful tool for global communication and exchange of information. The dependency of scholars in the academic knowledge resource centers on the e-resources has increased to a large extent. An information literature researcher could find it as convenient to make use of e-resources for his/her research work.

The E-resources facilitate the libraries to get the benefit of large number of resources at an affordable cost and in minimal time. Moreover, the digital technology has changed expectations of researchers, their patience and their willingness to accept services that are available on demand; the E-resources are the answer to expectations of the users.

The impact of Information Technology (IT) encourages the library user community to search information and to retrieve the required information. It also helps the knowledge economy by promoting Digital Knowledge Management (DKM) and objectively that the application of IT in the University library and information centers would certainly put an order and bring out a sequence of operations in Library and Information Management Environment (LISME) without much of human interventions.

1.2 DIGITAL KNOWLEDGE MANAGEMENT: AN OVERVIEW

Digital Knowledge Management is inevitable in the present digital technology era. It provides effective and efficient information and knowledge management services to the library user community in time on demand. The term knowledge management may be represented as a cross-disciplinary domain which can relate to a wide range of disciplines and technologies and some of which can include:

- Cognitive science
- Artificial Intelligence and Expert systems and Knowledge based Management Systems (KBMS)
- Groupware
- Library and information science
- Technical writing
- Documentation management
- Semantic Network
- Relational and object oriented database
- Simulation
- Management of information
- Management of people

1.2.1 Definitional Analysis of Digital Knowledge Management and ICT

The concept "Digital Knowledge Management (DKM)" may be defined as a tool for supporting the creation, archiving and sharing of valued information, expertise, and insight within and across communities of people and organizations with similar interests and needs to facilitate the web- based solutions to know-how the technologies on Digital/ Electronics learning towards organizational development. The term 'ICTs' may be defined as the use of hardware and software for efficient management of information, that is storage, retrieval, processing communication, diffusion and sharing of knowledge for socio-economic and cultural development.

1.2.2 Information and Knowledge

The term 'Information' may be defined as easy and quick approach to transfer information from one place to another and the term 'Knowledge' may be defined as slow to transfer knowledge from one person to another. The knowledge can be

- Explicit Knowledge
- Tacit knowledge
- Cultural Knowledge

The "Explicit Knowledge" can be easily described and specific enough to be documented and applied in education/training.

The "Tacit Knowledge" is harder to record and difficult to document or teach to others (heuristics often embedded in people's experiences and life's work). This is often the most elusive and most valuable type of knowledge. The different types of knowledge require different approaches to Knowledge Management (KM). Each presents unique challenges and opportunities.

The term 'Cultural Knowledge' may be defined as knowledge which includes assumptions and beliefs. It is used to understand, describe and explain the reality as well as conventions. It is also useful to form the framework among organizational members, recognize the new information and evaluate interpretations and actions.

1.2.3 Digital Electronic and Virtual Libraries

The concepts on Digital Electronic and Virtual Libraries as defined below in the following respects:

- The electronic library may be defined as a library that provides collections and or services in electronic form for example optical video disk, CD- ROM, online etc.
- The digital library may be defined a library that does not physically exist, most often used to denote a library with distributed collections or services that appear and act as one typical example is a web site with pointers to other sites.

1.2.4 E-learning

The term 'E-learning/digital learning' may be defined as the use of web-based technologies and applications for education and training combined approach with face to face classroom based teaching, education and training to the e-learning industry which includes organizations that support the establishment of learning infrastructures and networks for higher education institutions and corporations such as course management and delivery tools from Blackboard and WebCT that allow customers to create learning programmes directly on the web without investing in their own tools or infrastructure and some of the key characteristics of E-learning solutions can be identified towards organizations development.

- Relying on computer networking technologies so as to make it capable of instant updating storage/retrieval, distribution and sharing of instruction or information.
- Delivering to the learner via a computer that is connected to standard internet technologies.
- Focusing on the broadest view of learning moves on education and training and delivery of information and tools

to improve performance and competitiveness for information making aspects.

1.2.5 Digital Divide and E-Learning

The term "Digital divide" may be defined as the disparity between the 'haves' and the 'have-nots' for economic development and digital equality in the technology revolution for e-learning or otherwise the gap between the individuals, households, businesses, geographic areas at different socio-economic levels with regard to both their opportunities to access with ICTs (Information and Communication Technologies) and internet use in different activities towards rural sustainable development.

1.2.6 Information and Documentation Knowledge management Skills

The term 'Information and Documentation Knowledge Management' may be defined as the skills for information handling techniques such as acquisition, storage and control involved for knowledge dissemination and utilization of social capital resources management related e-information resources, products and services in information knowledge resource centers for rural community sustainable development.

From the above definitions, the following inferences have been made:

i. Digital Knowledge Management and ICT application knowledge resources are essential to manage the emerging amount of information being generated all over the world.

ii. The digital knowledge management and ICT applications tools are useful and relevant for online resources access facilities such as E-journals (Full text and bibliographies),

E-Books, online databases and website etc. in the Library and Information Centers (LICs) in the present e-knowledge society.

1.2.7 Perspectives on Knowledge, Information, Data

The Perspectives on Knowledge, Information, and Data indicated above in section (1.2.6), the pictorial representation as identified below in a vivid manner in relation to the concepts.

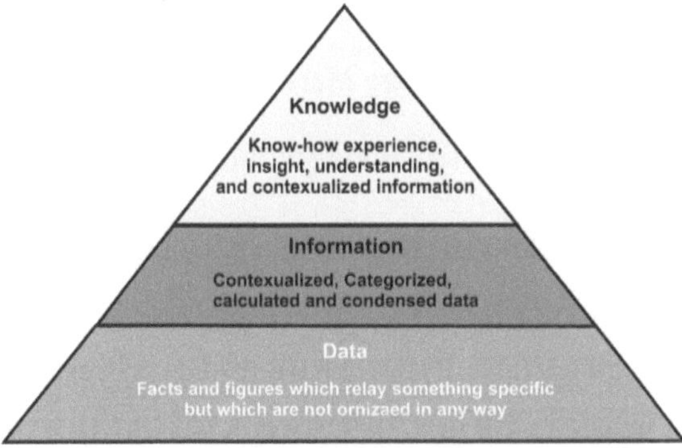

Figure 1.1 Perspectives on Knowledge, Information, and Data

Source: http://www.knowledge-management-tools.net/knowledge-information-data.html

1.2.8 The Dissemination of Knowledge Management Process Model (KMPM)

The Dissemination of Knowledge Management Process Model (KMPM) based on the innovative concept on "Knowledge Access and Sharing Information for Resources Approach Objectives **(KASIRAO)"** as indicated below, for knowledge sharing and dissemination towards organizational development in the present digital knowledge era.

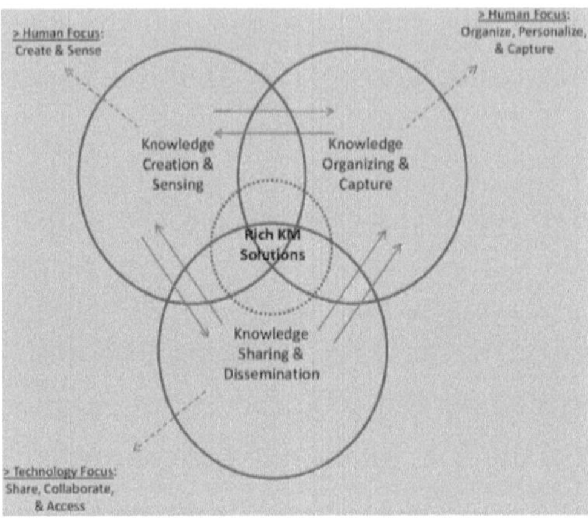

Figure 1.2 The Knowledge Management Process Model

Source : http://www.businessdictionary.com/definition/knowledge.html

1.2.9 Digital Knowledge Management AND Innovative Concept: Knowledge Access AND Sharing Information for Resources Approach Objectives (KASIRAO) in Education sectors towards Sustainable Development

Based on the impact of ICTs on organizational, social and economic relations, the 'Social and Educational Network Programs" such as E-Governance, E-Culture, E-Health, E-Learning, E-Education, E-Commerce, Audio and video method of communication handling techniques, delivery strategies and pedagogical skills for teachers and instructors in the class room teaching etc., are promoting in relation to the innovative concept "KASIRAO", through ICTs application tools in education sectors for societal development (Kasi Rao 2008).

The **new innovative formula** concept known as **K = 6A** to support its theory on **KASIRAO** for Millennium Development Goals **(MDGS)** in Education Sectors towards sustainable development. IPR obtained from Intellectual Property Management Division,

Council of Scientific and Industrial Research (CSIR), Government of India, New Delhi, Ref No. 024Cr2010 dated 15.11.2010. The theory and formula as highlighted below in Figure 1.3

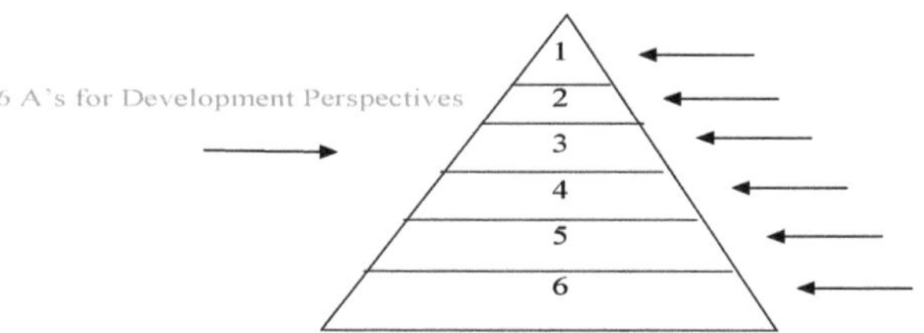

Figure 1.3 Knowledge Access amd Sharing Information for Resources Approach Objectives (KASIRAO)

1.2.10 Implications of Digital Knowledge Management and ICT in the University Library and Information Centers

The three stages have identified in the development of Information Communication Technology (ICT), the present digital knowledge environment the stage one portraits "Automated technology management", the second stage characteristics "Information resource management" and the third stage concern with "knowledge management" based on the conceptual analysis view, the Digital Knowledge Management (DKM) and ICT applications tools supporting for information storage, retrieval and dissemination systems and services in the library, information and documentation knowledge resources center for e-resources access to the library user community to fulfill their needs and demands in time (Kasi Rao 2009).

From the above implications, the following inferences have been made in relation to the advantages of E-resources:

i. E-resources provide user friendly interface.
ii. User can access information 24X7 hours with remote access facilities.
iii. E-resources can be access by several user simultaneity.
iv. Electronic resources have multidisciplinary approach.
v. E-resources provide advance searching tools.
vi. E-resources ignore missing issue problems.
vii. Article on electronic form can be also print as a hardcopy.
viii. Not required more timing for publishing and distributing Process.
ix. E-resources is upgrade then Print version.

1.3 PROPOSED RESEARCH

Digital revolution has transformed the intellectual function of traditional libraries. Digital libraries are providing the base for a set of distributed activities. It is also providing a one step solution for speedy delivery in a reliable fashion. Libraries are being digitized and patrons demand is growing the concept of content management has been adapted to the library world. More libraries are providing virtual references via the web.

The greatest challenge for the information manager today is to create an organization that can share knowledge. Quality library services are imperative in knowledge society as it inspires the knowledge workers to be innovative, viz. think globally and design locally. Today, information professionals have more opportunities to expand from their traditional role to organize the digital content, especially of getting and filtering available information which the information professionals are expected to be elevated from managing the corporate information center to managing corporate knowledge and become Chief Information Officers (CIO) and with greater responsibilities. These aspirations arising out of a belief that information professionals are best suited for the CIO's job since they already have the basic skills and attitude for such a job.

The expertise of information professionals in searching for and providing access to explicit knowledge in the form of documents, their skills in understanding clients needs, their knowledge of information sources and their skills in organizing information and developing databases have been core competencies used by organizations. From a Knowledge Management (KM) perspective, these skills are useful in helping professionals internalize explicit knowledge and also in facilitating the combination mode of knowledge conversion. New competencies are required to be developed to cope with the increasing emphasis on KM and several professional bodies such as ALA (American Library Association) and SLA (Special Library Association) have come up with the recommendations for this purpose.

"The core of the professional expertise of information professionals may be said to arise from a unique confluence of expertise in three areas, viz. knowledge of information sources, knowledge of users and knowledge of the application of information technologies for the benefit of users and for the management of information resources".

The recognition of the vital role LISS (Library, Information Systems and Services in India) could play in the educational, scientific, industrial and overall socio-economic development of India began to receive acceptance only after independence in 1947, when the government embarked upon several programs of national development and reconstruction.

The need for developing these systems and services became all the more essential because of certain factors such as vast proliferation's in the universe of information and knowledge and the resultant document/information explosion in the world and the varied and complex needs of users for information in R&D activities, educational and research programs and various other fields of human activities. As a result, a fairly large infrastructure of LISS has been developed in the country during the past five decades or so. Though much remains to be done in this field yet the achievements already made can largely be considered as commendable providing an optimistic basis for the future.

Besides the developments in different types of libraries, documentation/information centers, bibliographical services, etc., library and information networks at local level such as DELNET and CALIBNET and at the national level such as ENVIS, NISSAT and INFLIBNET and others are being developed. Access through information networks such as NICNET, ERNET, SIRNET, NKN, NDL, SWAYAM and INDONET and several others is being utilized in the LISS in the country for services such as CAS, SDI, Internet facilities are being used in many libraries and information systems for benefit of the users.

The future library operations and information services are tending towards remarkable changes. In addition to managing the traditional media, a sizable volume of information has to be handled in electronic form. In the context of university libraries, the electronic media outweigh the traditional media. These developments warrant the library and information centers to adopt KM and IT to compete with the changing dimensions and trends in the provision of information services according to the changing needs of the users.

In recent years, the applications of ICT in library and information centers in India has been in rapid speed due to the impact of emerging networks at local, regional and national level and also the availability of information in digital form and the recent establishment of Anna University Library has triggered the applications of ICT in library and information centers in and around Chennai. Added to this, information seekers are more conscious in seeking/searching information digitally. Taking these factors into consideration, it is proposed to study the nature and extent of Digital Knowledge Management and ICT applications in the University Library and Information Centers. Hence, this proposed research.

1.4 STATEMENT OF THE RESEARCH TITLE

"Digital Knowledge Management in the University Library and Information Centers in Chennai (Madras): An Analytical Study".

1.4.1 Explanation of the Concepts

1.4.1.1 Digital Knowledge Management and ICT The concept "Digital Knowledge Management (DKM)" may be defined as a tool for supporting the creation, archiving and sharing of valued information, expertise, and insight within and across communities of people and organizations with similar interests and needs to facilitate the web- based solutions to know-how the technologies on Digital/Electronics learning towards organizational development.

The term 'ICTs' may be defined as the use of hardware and software for efficient management of information, that is storage, retrieval, processing communication, diffusion and sharing of knowledge for socio-economic and cultural development. (More account on Digital Knowledge Management (DKM)" has been given in the Section 1.2)

1.4.1.2 University Library and Information centers in Chennai In the city of Chennai, there are about 24 university library and information centers comprising of State, Central and Deemed Universities are considered for the study.

1.5 OBJECTIVES

The study has been conducted with the following objectives:

i. To survey the University Library and Information centers on Digital Knowledge Management and ICT applications in and around Chennai(Madras).
ii. To study the nature of Digital Knowledge Management Resource access facilities in libraries under survey.
iii. To examine the availability of digital knowledge management information products and services.
iv. To analyze the impact of Digital Knowledge Management on collection development and professional development in Library and Information Centers.
v. To elicit the opinion of the Library user community and LIS professionals on digital knowledge management resources access facilities in the University Library and Information Centers.
vi. To identify the constraints, if any, towards digital knowledge management resources access facilities in the University Library and Information Centers.
vii. To offer suggestions for effective implementation of ICT applications tools for digital knowledge management services in the Library and Information Centers (Kasi Rao 2007).

1.6 HYPOTHESES

Based on the observations, the following hypotheses were framed: -

i. Majority of the university library and information centers in Chennai have implemented ICT application tools for the provision of Digital Knowledge Management (DKM) information products and services.
ii. Application of ICT is more prominent in State University libraries than the Deemed University libraries.
iii. Among the Central and Deemed University libraries, the State University libraries are in better position in the adoption of ICT in Digital Knowledge Management services.
iv. Majority of the University libraries and Information Centers are using commercially developed library software packages.
v. There is an increasing trend in the provision of DKM information products and services.
vi. The concept of resource sharing is not much prevalent/common among the library and information centers.
vii. The ICT serves as a tool in the Collection Development Policy (CDP) programs in the library and information centers under survey.
viii. The application of Information and Communication Technology (ICT) influences the man power planning and development in library and information centers.
ix. Library staff has passive attitude towards ICT applications towards DKM services in library and information centers.
x. Factors like lack of finance, lack of training etc. hinder the promotion of ICT in library and information centers under survey.

1.7 SIGNIFICANCE

The study is significant in the following respects:

i. The study of this nature brings the state-of-the–Art of the University Library and Information Centers in Chennai, projecting the Digital Knowledge Management (DKM) services.
ii. It also examines a comparison of ICT application in State and Deemed University library and information centers.
iii. Results of the study would influence the top management so as to strengthen/streamline the existing set-up of library operation.
iv. This study would pave the way to conduct similar studies in other geographical territories.

1.8 LIMITATIONS

i. The research study excludes the library and information centers, which do not have application of ICT and Digital Knowledge Management information products and services.
ii. The opinions/views are from the Head of the Library and Information Centers and the library user community are considered and not from the other staff.
iii. It does not cover the public and school libraries.

1.9 METHODOLOGY

The research design/methodology involves in the following respects:

The literature on "Digital Knowledge Management and Information needs and seeking behavior of the user community in the Library and Information Centers" has to study and review for facilitating the questionnaire construction. The Questionnaire method serves as tool to collect data from the Librarian, Faculty Members, Research Scholars in the University Library and Information Centers.

Step 1: Review of Literature

The literature on Digital Knowledge Management (DKM) and Information and Communication Technology (ICT) and its application in Library and Information Centers (LICs) has been studied and reviewed, which facilitated the construction of questionnaire.

Step 2: Questionnaire Construction

Based on the review of literature, a structured questionnaire (Appendix-A and B) have been designed to collect data from the target library and information centers. The questionnaire covers information in the following seven sections.

Section I: Profile of the University library and information centers

Elicits information pertaining to the profile and library and information centers, such as location, year of establishment, holdings of the library types of services offered and quantum of users

Section II: Areas of Digital Knowledge Management and ICT applications

Covers application of Digital Knowledge Management (DKM) in various sections of the library and the provision of database services and products. It also covers the provision of technology-based facilities such as reprography, consortium and networking.

Section III: Purpose of Digital Library and use of ICT Applications

Elicits information on impact of DKM and ICT applications on collection development activities of libraries and information centers.

Section IV: Attitude towards Digital Library and ICT Application

Deals with application of DKM and ICT centers influence the personnel management policies and also leads to professional advancement.

Section V: Digital Collection towards Development and ICT Application

Elicit attitudes of the librarians towards DKM and ICT applications

Section VI : Digital Knowledge Management Software Applications AND Professional Development

Identifies the reasons for poor DKM and ICT application in library and information centers under survey.

Section VII : Reasons for Poor Digital Knowledge Management for Digital Libraries

Identifies the reasons for poor Digital Knowledge Management in library information centres under survey.

Step 3: Questionnaire Survey

3.1 Pilot Study

A Pilot study was conducted with a sample of six university library and information centers and the results were tested. Based on the study, the questionnaire was further modified and developed to suit the stated objectives. Accordingly, revised version of the questionnaire was fully developed.

3.2 Administration of the questionnaire

The revised questionnaire was administered among 24 university library and information centers in and around Chennai where the applications of DKM and ICT are evident. A total number of 2400 questionnaire were distributed and responded 2057, the respond rate is 86%. The respondents comprises of State, Central and Deemed University libraries.

Step 4: Observation and Interview Method

Besides, collecting data through questionnaire, the investigator has taken an effort to visit the University library and information centers to observe the extent of DKM facilities. This is followed by the unstructured and informal interview with the librarians of the respective universities.

Step 5 : Data Analysis

The data collected from the questionnaire has been analyzed to test the hypothesis framed and to fulfill the stated objectives. For this purpose SPSS software package has been used for the statistical analysis techniques such as Mean, Median, Mode, Standard Deviation, Clustering analysis and Proximity Matrix etc. depending on the nature of the data collected from the respondents.

1.10 MAJOR FINDINGS

1. It is found that application of digital knowledge management is mostly seen in the state university libraries. Among the central university libraries and deemed university libraries have evinced interest in digital knowledge management and ICT applications.
2. Different types of services are being provided by the libraries under survey, which are broadly grouped as traditional, documentation and ICT based services.
3. Majority of the libraries used commercial developed software packages.
4. It is found that a small proportion of staff are deputed for various professional advanced programs.
5. The applications of DKM and ICT have an impact on Collection Development Policy and professional Development Policy.

6. Libraries have positive attitude towards application of DKM and ICT. The staff in university libraries has shown a higher degree of positive attitude towards DKM and ICT.
7. However certain barriers such as insufficient funds, lack of adequate trained staff, lack of coordination, initiative on the part of library professionals and fear of modern information technology etc., have been identified that come in the way of DKM applications.

1.11 MAJOR SUGGESTIONS

1. It is suggested that university library and information officers shall strive a right choice between printed and electronic resources of publication.
2. It is suggested that the internet based services such as e-mail shall be made available to the clientele of the libraries, as being provided by the libraries in the West.
3. It is suggested that the library and information centers in Chennai shall share the resources both textual and bibliographic data.
4. It is suggested that launching the under mentioned programmes to achieve the goals of man power development in the ICT era.
   - Recruitment of expertise in DKM and ICT.
   - Establishment of Digital Knowledge Centers.
   - Establishment of audio-visual and teleconference centers.
5. It is suggested that National Task Force(NTF) shall be implemented in action plan to motivate the LIS professionals.
   - Design and development of Mobile-OPAC and SMS alerts.
   - University library is to establish the digital knowledge center and spoken tutorial centers.
   - RFID technology and QR code technologies.
   - Social network and resource sharing services to the library users.

6. It is suggested that the need of joining in a National Knowledge Network (NKN), NPTEL, SWAYAM and NDL to the university libraries.
    - Internet based Digital knowledge management services to the university libraries.
    - Internet based Research support services to the university libraries.
7. It is suggested that the implementation of e-learning resource materials to the university libraries
    - The implementation of multimedia literature materials to the university libraries.
    - The implementation of digital reference services .
    - The implementation of federated search engine facility to the university libraries.
    - Remote access facilities to the university library users.
    - The implementation of Digital notice board to the user communities.
    - Use of Cloud computing facilities to the User communities in the libraries
    - The Memorandum of Understanding (MoU) with the foreign university library for the technological access facilities and services

1.12 CONSPECTUS

The thesis has been presented in six chapters.

Chapter1 Introduces the concept of Digital Knowledge Management (DKM) and Information Communication Technology(ICT). Presents the need for the proposed research in the University Libraries and Information Centers. Further, it highlights objectives, Hypotheses, Limitations, Significance and methodology adopted.

Chapter 2 Brings the review of the related literature

Chapter 3 Provides an overview of the university libraries and information centers in Chennai, under survey.

Chapter 4 Discusses the results of the analysis and interpretations of the data collected through questionnaire on Digital Knowledge Management and ICT applications in the University library and information centers. In addition to differential analysis is in terms of advanced SPSS statistical techniques such as, Mean, Standard Deviation, Median, Mode, clustering analysis and Proximity Matrix. Besides presenting the data in a tabular form, graphical presentation such as pie chart, bar diagram and linear graph have also been used.

Chapter 5 Lists the summary of major findings and observations.

Chapter 6 Offers suggestions and recommendations based on the study and identifies the areas for further research.

The thesis concludes with a list of bibliographic references and appendices.

Chapter II

REVIEW OF LITERATURE

2.1 INTRODUCTION

In this chapter an attempt is made to review the literature on Digital Knowledge Management and the University library and information centers in order to provide comprehensive conceptualization, the literature reviewed has been categorized under the following broad headings:

i. The studies on the role of Digital Knowledge Management and ICT application in the University Library and Information Centers.
ii. The studies on the need for Information and Communication Technology (ICT) application in the Library and Information Centers.
iii. The studies on various issue/problems in Digital Knowledge Management and ICT application.
iv. The studies on planning strategies in Digital Knowledge Management and ICT application.
v. The attitudes of library staff towards Digital Knowledge Management and ICT application.

2.2 ROLE OF DIGITAL KNOWLEDGE MANAGEMENT AND ICT APPLICATION IN THE UNIVERSITY LIBRARY and INFORMATION CENTERS

Paulin and Sunesan (2012) in their study have highlighted the significance of Digital Knowledge Management in Library and Information Centers and discussed the views on knowledge management such as knowledge transfer, knowledge sharing and knowledge barriers. The study concludes by highlighting the concepts on knowledge as an object and subject content for its effectiveness in the information management activities in the library and information centers.

Pawlowski and Bick (2012) in their study, on the concept of Global Knowledge Management (GKM) have attempted to describe the components and influencing factors on knowledge management processes and systems and can be used for two main purposes. On the one hand, it guides development processes by providing a solution space and success factors for decision makers as well as implementers. On the other hand, it is a reference for researchers to compare research in the field by providing a common set of context descriptions as well as aspects influencing the success of knowledge management solutions.

Gururaj et al. (2012) have stated that the development of Knowledge Management (KM) in recent years has become the key concern for librarians and libraries. They have highlighted the importance of knowledge management in the 21st Century and emphasized the need for Knowledge Management (KM), Knowledge Management implementation and other concepts.

Gururaj (2012) has analyzed the Impact on Knowledge Management (IKM) in Library and Information Centers (LICs) and found that the IKM in LICs are essential. Further, this study has emphasized the need for KM for information marketing in the present digital knowledge society.

Thiyam Satyabati Devi and Nomsa Mathebala (2012) very strongly stress the necessity of regularly meeting for discussing the business of the library for achieving its overall goals. Aims for the identification of the management problems of the library. It examines the existing management environment, outlines the user expectations and offer suggestions for enhanced control of the Information. It examines the modulus and process of management and discusses the technique.

Walter et al (2010) suggests the effectiveness of KM as an increasingly important source of competitive advantage and a key to the success of contemporary organizations, to support the employees for collective expertise towards organizational development. Propose a conceptual framework for using ICT to enhance KM in higher education and identify a research agenda to bridge the requirements of theory building and testing, to address the different emerging challenges. Conceptualize an organization in the proposed ICT framework as a knowledge space, as required by the organization.

Jasmina (2011) suggests that the introduction of knowledge management in higher education is inevitable, due to the current social and economic changes in the knowledge economy in higher institutions for knowledge management process and culture towards institutional development.

Guodong Ni (2010) studied the Vicarious Management Corporation (VMC) and Knowledge Management (KM) and discussed the contents of the knowledge management of the VMC and obtained the knowledge management model to establish the knowledge management system to build the virtual-learning knowledge management organization, develop the learning organization culture, stipulate for the sound knowledge management rules and regulations, pay attention to carry out the incentive of spirit and competition within the organization, build efficient information platform for knowledge management and constantly improve the level of knowledge management through the performance evaluation for knowledge management.

Gurjeet Kaur Rattan, Saroj Bala (2013) study identified the use of information resources and services at Punjab University Extension Library in Mohali. Further, the study discussed a few suggestions to make the services more beneficial for the library user community at large.

Sohini Sengupta Ray and Dibyendu Paul (2013) the study has focused the gender division in LIS profession in the perspective of ICT environment. Address three sets of relationships like profession and technology; profession and gender; and the technology and gender to evaluate women's participation in LIS profession in the current day's perspectives.

Ashish Kumar Pal (2014) described Digital Rights Management (DRM) is emerging as a formidable new challenges and focuses on security like encryption and watermarking.

Iqbal Bhat, Mahesh V. Mudhol (2014) presented the findings of a survey about the awareness and use of electronic resources by medical students available in the medical institute libraries. Presented and discussed the results of this survey.

Rekha D. Pai, and Sagender Singh Parmar (2015) described the elaborative study on Manipal University Digital Repository (MUDR) and its collection growth. Presented some suggestions that can be implemented to improve the strength and visibility of MUDR which can be equally applicable to any institutional repository.

Mohamed Haneefa and Syamili (2014) aimed for the investigation of use of Information and Communication Technology

(ICT) by the visually impaired students in Calicut University, Kerala. The study found that a large majority of the students are computer literates and use mobile phones frequently.

Akhtar Hussain and Parvez Ahmad (2014) aimed for the discussion of social media by online newspapers in Saudi Arabia. The findings of this can be utilized to assess the status of assorted web 2.0 tools used in online newspapers. The paper begins with an introduction to Saudi Arabia's education and media technology and further attempts to define and explain to web 2.0 applications which are useful to the online newspapers.

Kailash Chandra Das, ed.al (2014) aimed for the evaluation of the existing positions of Post Graduate(PG) college libraries under University of Kerala and to find out from users point of view identified the technology-aided services are provided and their impact on quality of services. The key purpose of this study is to assess the users rating of the quality of library service. Some of the key findings of this study are there exists a significant difference between male and female post graduated college students in their levels of satisfaction of users of various services provided in the post graduate library.

Padma, Ramasamy and Niramathi (2015) attempted to examine some of the features that appear in the debates around the nature and methodologies of a discipline that is still forming, i.e. the digital humanities, in order to identify the types of lessons that can be learnt by information science from this study.

Anil Kumar Dhiman and Mandan Lal Jat (2014) discussed the knowledge management concept, importance of knowledge management in education sector especially traditional colleges in Pune City, strategies used to capture students, teachers and processes knowledge and suggested knowledge management process for traditional higher educational institute based on the survey conducted. This article will be useful to all educational institutes who are interested to practice and apply knowledge management process.

Beth Guay, et al. (2014) their survey informed metadata services departments about the management of constantly changing electronic resources cataloging workflows and also discussed cataloging workflow as it pertains to Electronic Resources Management System (ERMS) development.

Abdul Mannan Khan (2011) aimed to find out the availability and utilization level of CD-ROM databases in IIT Kharagpur library. Revealed that most of the user consult with CD ROM databases not only for updating their knowledge but also for collecting relevant information for the study and research purposes.

Noushia (2011) explored social networking site (SNS). Reported the survey of social networking site, Facebook in making awareness among LIS professionals. This analysis will help the LIS professionals to deriving the benefits of SNS for networking and resource sharing benefits and the quality management services in library and information centers.

Rajashekara (2017) Information explosion and rapid growth in technology made the existing knowledge of software technology library professionals ineffective, which they had at the time of entering into the organization. Hence, professionals have to be trained to operate new techniques and equipment's, to handle the present as well as new jobs more effectively. Training is useful not only for the organizations, but also for the employees as it develops knowledge, problem-solving ability and skill of the newly recruited employees on the one hand and serves as a refresher course in updating old employees on the other hand. It aims at improving the organization's performance through the enhanced performance of its employees. Because of these reasons training has become an integral part of human resource development in software technology libraries. Knowing this fact following study has been conducted to identify the training and development facilities provided to in Indian software technology libraries.

2.3 NEED FOR INFORMATION AND COMMUNICATION TECHNOLOGY (ICT) APPLICATION IN THE UNIVERSITY LIBRARY AND INFORMATION CENTERS

Fatma (2010) suggested that Knowledge Management is the core subject of organizations in today's challenging world and a major focus of knowledge management is on transforming tacit knowledge into an explicit one. Since knowledge is constituted in individuals and depends on individual experiences, institutions, insight and personal judgment, it is difficult to capture.

If it is extracted, it may be codified and become a tangible form of knowledge. Otherwise, it is called as tacit knowledge. Since codified knowledge is easy to be shared and used, it is emphasized that the knowledge which provides a competitive advantage is a tacit one and tacit knowledge is seen as a strategic asset for the competitive advantage and sustainability of organizations.

Singh and Nazim, Mohammad (2008) Information technology is currently taking center stage and transformed the whole world into a global village with a global economy, which is increasingly dependent on the creative management and distribution of information. The enormous advantages it has in easing the delivery of information around the world. The paper discusses the impact of information technology and role of libraries in the age of knowledge and information societies. It also highlights the problems faced by the Library & Information Service (LIS) sector in India and achievements over the years using modern information technologies.

Jayadev Kadli and Kumbar (2011) stated that changing technologies have brought a more sophisticated and higher spread of communication. Academic libraries were responding to this change in the learning and research environment and ICT changed the behavior of library users.

Li He (2008) elicited that the Knowledge Management (KM) in Digital Library should include Knowledge-oriented management, Human-oriented management and Ability-oriented management as the emphasis formation parts, on the basis of the study on essential theory of KM in Digital Library (DL). Then, designing the pattern of KM in DL from the three levels such as knowledge resources management, human resources management and organizational construction in the web knowledge society.

Anaraki (2011) stated that the Digital libraries (DLs) and e-learning systems are the important enabling technologies for the knowledge supply chain in the digital age. Therefore, she addresses the meaning of "e learning" and how it can be supported by the digital library environment, the functionality of the digital library and how e-learning resources are included and organized in the digital library. Aimed to examine and discuss the crucial roles libraries play in e-learning; the challenges and opportunities facing the e-learning program and the library's involvement.

Proposed a model for implementing e-learning through DLs according to knowledge management process. The proposed model would contribute to the advancement of academic debate in both the areas of DL and e-learning.

Arlitsch, Kenning & Sadler, Shawna (2015) have focused on the footsteps and provided a roadmap for embarking on the construction of a new technologically advanced library building.

Sarojadevi and Padmamma (2013) dealt with the existing patterns of collection and acquisition, its organization, management and retrieval of information resources preserved in the library. The information is usually stored, but more important is to organize the collection on such a way that needed information can be retrieved immediately.

Pardeep Rattan (2013) studied the usage of Information Communication Technology (ICT) products and services implemented in the libraries of government engineering colleges in the state of Punjab.

Md. Sohail, Andleeb Alvi (2014) described the use of web resources (e-journals and e-databases) subscribed by UGC-Infonet consortium) by the students of medical sciences at Aligarh Muslim University, India. Indicated that it is probably counter-productive to evaluate students as one group. Different segments of students have very different and varied use patterns of web resources depending on study top, study year, psychological dispositions and other demographic factors.

Sangeetha N. Dhamdhere (2015) discussed the purpose of using e-resources offered by University Grant Commission(UGC) Info net-consortium, advantages and barriers of e-resources, preferred file formats and sources of using e-resources. Besides studying the use of UGC-info net consortium. Examined the utilization and satisfaction levels of users with respect to the e-resources.

Anjali Verma, et al. (2015) highlighted the Definitions, Characteristics, Key Features, Concepts, Principles, Applications, Learning Mode, Technologies, Implementing, Web 2.0 Applications used for LIS Services, Purposes, Library 2.0, Ten Web 2.0 Tools, Directory, Advantages, Benefits and General Issues. Skills of Librarians 2.0, Traditional Roles, User Expectations, List of Experts and so on.

Arne J. Almquist (2014) provided an explanation of the marketing concept and orientation contrasted with the much more common production orientation. Illustrated the concepts through models and a description of the marketing effort as it has developed.

Joe J Marquez (2012) a case study on the implementation of an online timeline, the Sonoma County Timeline â, which was used to showcase the library's resources at Sonoma State University. Demonstrated how to build a timeline can be used to extend the library's presence to its community. Detailed a guide to managing the project, a status report for the Sonoma State University Libraries instance of Exhibit and a discussion of best practices.

Saikat, Goswami (2011) aimed a movement for encouraging and enabling sharing content freely called Open Educational Resources (OER) for the reason of rapidly changing in all the aspects of information technologies in modern information era.

Ahmad Parvez (2011) the study has highlighted the impact of ICT on products & services in library and information centers. Further, the study has emphasized the need for library automation, digital archives and mobile phone information services to meet the user needs in the present digital knowledge environment.

Ramakrishna et al. (2015) the study has focused on online resources in selected Deemed University libraries of Andhra Pradesh, India. This study has also attempted to present comprehensive and up to date information about the number of online resources subscribed and the number of online resources available in the

University libraries. Further, study suggested that the online resource access facilities are essential in a library information center to strengthen the existing library services.

2.4 THE STUDIES ON PLANNING STRATEGIES IN DIGITAL KNOWLEDGE MANAGEMENT AND ICT APPLICATION

Nath, Bahl and Kumar (2007) reported a survey of librarians of Chandigarh to assess the way in which librarians use ICTs, their level of knowledge and skills, problems faced in the use of ICTs and their training needs. Investigated the extent of adoption of ICT in Chandigarh libraries as modern tools of providing library service to users.

Baker and Shirley (2007) stated that the libraries are faced with great opportunities to take responsibility for digital information and knowledge management, both on their campuses and across disciplines. These opportunities come, however, with significant challenges. The challenges are less technical than they are financial and social-identifying funding and penetrating the facility culture to generate enthusiasm and support for sustainable work.

Shabahat Husain and Mohammad Nazim (2013) aimed to identify, collect and critically review the research literature on the concepts of Knowledge Management (KM) among Library & Information Science(LIS) professionals on the basis of the review of published work in the field of KM and librarianship. Provided a theoretical foundation for further research to investigate the problems and prospects of implementing KM in libraries. Virtual learning environment became very popular in the present learning environment. Endeavored to discuss the experiences of the administrator, teachers and also the ultimate users with the present study.

Gareema Sanamanand Shailendra Kumar (2014) aimed to examine the user's awareness and satisfaction level with the available Assistive Technology (AT) facilities for the people with disabilities in National Capital Region (NCR) libraries of India. Depicted lack of at facilities in NCR libraries of India. Majority of users are 'Not satisfied' with available AT facilities and face various barriers in the use of AT in NCR libraries.

This study proved it as useful for the LIS professionals and the research community to provide an insight into the current status of the AT available in NCR libraries in India. This study had first explored the viewpoint of people with disabilities regarding the ATs that are available in NCR libraries of India.

Pravish Prakash and Ashwani Kumar (2015) aimed to explore the status of information literacy skills of students of universities of Punjab & Chandigarh, their information seeking strategies and ability in acquiring, organizing, evaluating and using the information effectively. Put some suggestions based on the findings. Expected that the assessment of information literacy competency of students would go a long way towards creating an information literate society and it would also provide some insight to researchers for future evaluation and planning.

Bridget Schumacher and Dean Hendrix (2012) recommended the establishment of a communication plan for creating a more cohesive online presence. Stated that this study article is an account of the University Libraries within the State University of New York and at Bullalas early experiences with screen casting, assessment of screen casting services and the consequent development of a coherent communications plan and best practices document regarding video and screencast production.

Samantha Schmehl Hines and Eric Hines (2012) described a case study using a collaborative model of problem-based learning in library instruction as an innovative alternative to traditional methods. Examined the results of the assignment students were given as part of the exercise. They found that the problem-based learning model increased student engagement with library resources and provided a mechanism for identifying and correcting deficiencies in students' information literacy knowledge and skills. It is realized that if a specific session of library instruction is intended to provide guidance on the use of the library for a particular assignment or project, then using a problem-based learning approach in collaboration with teaching faculty is a simple way to improve library instruction.

Shelley Arlen et al. (2014) discussed the planning and creative processes involved in producing tutorials that address an identified instructional need using new technologies and a storytelling model. Also addressed are copyright issues, finding public domain images and working with a production partner that is independent of the library. The videos described here were created to help students and others understand the differences between primary and secondary documents using a storyline based on the popular topic of pirates.

Carmen Mitchell and Melanie Chu (2014) stated that the data from this survey and examination of current campus climate, combined with the analysis of implementation factors by other organizations, will bolster the argument for libraries to create open repositories for campus scholarship.

Karel Sobel, Jeffrey Beall (2011) examined the problem of linguistic change in humanities research in full-text databases and described the innovative solution offered by two proprietary library content providers.

Jody L. DeRidder (2011) described the Project related knowledge resources at the University of Alabama Libraries which seeks to recreate the patron experience in the reading room via the Web. This project tested a model for lowering the costs of Web delivery of large collections using folder level descriptions.

2.5 PLANNING STRATEGIES IN KNOWLEDGE MANAGEMENT AND ICT APPLICATION

Das, Dutta and Sen (2007) assessed the present situation in the development of indigenous digital libraries focusing on the retrieval features of eight digital libraries in India. This study had shown that information retrieval features of digital libraries very significantly from each other due to the use of different content-organization techniques and differing types of digital content.

Ramesh Babu, et al. (2007) reported a survey of the Information and Communication Technology (ICT) skills among librarians in engineering educational institutions in Tamil Nadu with the main aim of identifying the types of ICT skills processed by the librarians. The knowledge in ICT is related to operating systems, packages and programming languages, library automation software, web awareness, knowledge of online facilities/services and also technical skills and managerial skills.

Sampath Kumar and Biradar (2010) examined the use of ICT in 31 college libraries in Karnataka, India by investigating the ICT infrastructure, current status of library automation, barriers to implementation of library automation and also librarians attitudes towards the use of ICT.

Dhanavandan et al. (2011) aimed at analyzing the use and availability of ICT infrastructure facilities in self-financing engineering college libraries in Tamil Nadu, which need rapid ICT infrastructure and adequate development of electronic resources. This study traced out the nature of electronic resources, library automation level, computerized library services, electronic access points, and type of digital libraries, network and topology of network, internet and intranet services with reference to the selected institutions.

Zhonghai Yu (2010) described the Digital design of mechanical products depends on reuse of existing design knowledge. Proposed an ontology based knowledge management approach and reuse method towards digital design process. Discussed the generic technology of the design knowledge management according to the characteristics of digital design process of mechanical products and the characteristics of knowledge reuse during them. Classified the digital design tasks into two basic types in the approach namely structure design and parametric design. Represented the relations between the design task and its knowledge linkage (design cases, design rules, design criteria and handbooks) in the ontology model. Through finding the linkage knowledge according to the current scenario of design phase, the relevant knowledge items would thus be effectively located and retrieved. A case of the digital design process of a thread rolling board illustrates the proposed approach.

Yuan Zhen (2010) analyzed mainly the current situation of building the digital library, explained the theory of knowledge management in the digital library and probed into the strategies of the digital library that applying knowledge management. Following four aspects are the key contents in this paper.

Tjicka & Liauw Toong (2007) discussed Petra Christian University Library's development on institutional repository and knowledge management in Surabaya, Indonesia. The digital library project specifically aimed to digitize, collect and disseminate indigenous knowledge. It stated that the development of DesaInformasi had positively affected school campuses because it had motivated the production of better works and had provided more awareness on copyright issues. Meanwhile, it asserted the capability of digital libraries to influence and strengthen the roles of libraries in the society.

Catherine Bailey and Martin Clarke, (2001) the study has highlighted the importance of Knowledge Management (KM) in the higher learning educational institutions. Further, the study has emphasized the need for decision making policy to support the managerial roles and responsibilities in an effective manner towards organizational development.

Jian-Hua YehJia-Yang Chang (2000) discussed the design of a digital library that addressed both content and knowledge management. The Structure of the two-tier repository System such as organization of temporal knowledge in the National Taiwan University Digital Library and Museum and Information extraction and the process of deriving implied knowledge.

Seema Vasishta (2013) presented a case study of strategic planning for managing electronic resources at Punjab Engineering College (PEC) University of Technology. Besides giving a brief account of historical development of PEC University of Technology, this research theme provided an overview of how access to electronic resources is being provided at the PEC Library. It also had shown how change from print-based resources to a hybrid (consisting of a mix of print and electronic) collection is being used for imparting information using technology as a catalyst.

Mehar Singh and Ashok Kumar (2013) libraries are not only acquiring printed material but also providing various learning resources in digital form. The present research article deals with the online digital resources, advantage and needs of preservation, infrastructure required for preservation in Indian environment.

Sivakumar and Dominic (2013) attempted to make the readers to understand the importance of Total Quality Management (TQM), an effective system that could enhance the performance of academic libraries with the aid of earlier research and literatures.

Madurai Meenachi and Sai Baba (2014) reported about the development of the portal for fast breeder test reactor (FBTR). Described about the methodology adopted for the development of the portal. Formats like RDF (Resource Description Framework), WOL (Web Ontology Language), Graphs, UML (Unified Modeling Language) were used to represent nuclear reactor knowledge.

Pravish Prakash and Ashwani Kumar (2015) aimed for the investigation of the factors that affect the optimum use and utilization of internet by research scholars at Banaras Hindu University, Varanasi. The study mainly focused on the preferred information sources in brief. The objectives, scope, research methodology of the study are clearly expanded. To conduct this kind of study the researchers prepared a well-structured questionnaire as a tool for data collection and same response were subjected to mathematical and statistical analysis.

Ayodele Smart Obajemu (2013) There is an eagerness on the part of librarians and libraries in Nigeria to shift from traditional methods of information representation to modern information technologies. This has led to the influx of various library software into the ICT market to drive automation needs of libraries. There is the need, however, for quality and reliable software that can effectively run on the operating systems of computers in Nigerian libraries. Therefore, this study aimed to create awareness of the existing software in Nigeria so as to enhance quality selection. It provided librarians with pragmatic steps to take when making choices and highlights the operational problems associated with library software. Results of the survey had shown that a greater number of the respondents are computer literate, and agree with the guiding steps a library should follow before acquiring software. The study not only discussed the problems associated with software installations but also suggested ways out of them. Finally, the study made the recommendations on the way forward.

Uta Hussong-Christian et al. (2013) Key findings confirmed that trialing new technology is crucial to determining if the technology fits an individual's needs and is necessary to inform the development of library services and professional knowledge.

Jon Jeffreyes, et al (2011)[66] reported on educational technology by the research group at the University of Minnesota, Twin Cities examined the educational technology used in courses and then identified a method to effectively integrate library resources with existing course technologies. The group developed a plan for a library course page system that automatically generates a page populated with relevant library resources for each class.

2.6 LIBRARY STAFF ATTITUDES TOWARDS DIGITAL KNOWLEDGE MANAGEMENT AND ICT APPLICATION

Nav Jyoti Dhingra (2013) assessed the attitudes towards e-journals available through Consortium for E-Resources in Agriculture (CERA)-Consortium and examined the current level of use of these electronic publications by faculty members of the Punjab Agricultural University, Ludhiana. Conducted a survey by using questionnaire to collect data. Attempted to define this consortium, its objectives and scope also. Explored that usage of e-journals has increased as compared to the printed journals as majority of users have started accepting the journals in electronic form. Faculty is accessing these-journals at their concerned departments more as compared to the library. Presented their responses and remarks.

Anna Kaushik (2013) aimed to obtain perception and feedback of Library and Information Science (LIS) marketing professionals regarding marketing activities, searching and finding internet resources on marketing of library services area through online questionnaire. The results of this study revealed that in "Marketing Library Service", Google and Yahoo emerged as most effective search term and search engine for searching and finding information on marketing of library services on Internet. This study would be helpful for information seekers and LIS professionals in order to identify search patterns and usefulness of internet resources available on marketing of library services area.

Ngozi Blessing Ukachi et al. (2014) focused on the examining the extent of use and the attitude of Under Graduate (UG) students towards the use of Electronic Information Resources (EIRs). It aimed to establish the relationship between UG students attitude and their use of EIRs in university libraries in South-West, Nigeria.

Thanuskodi (2014) presented the results of a survey of the post graduate students of the Bharadhidasan University, Tamil Nadu with the aim of exploring the Internet use behavior of students.

Mohd Muzzammil, Mehtab Alam Ansari (2014) recommended that the seminar library professionals should be provided with more chances of formal training to introduce all possible ICT-based resources and services that can improve their ICT literacy. Moreover, this study emphasized the need for redesigning the course curriculum of library and information science curriculum in universities of India supporting the appropriate skills and expertise to be able to handle the application of ICT.

Sharad Kumar Sonker, et al. (2015) attempted to trace out the awareness and use of e-resources by the full time Ph.D. scholars of four departments of School of Chemistry at Madurai Kamaraj University, Madurai.

Curtis Brundy (2015) reviewed the literature on academic libraries and innovations. The information presented would assist library readers in making decisions that affect innovation and would highlight areas for further research.

Amanda Melcher, Kathleen Lowe (2014) described a learning exercise for an English composition information literacy instruction session that merges technology with active learning and is fun and engaging. Librarians introduced digital cameras into library instruction.

Diane VanderPol, Emily A.B. Swanson (2013) described the experience of librarians at Westminster College leading a faculty and staff Learning Community that addressed the information literacy elements such as some of the more complex learning outcomes in standards three and four, such as the students ability to synthesize and use information to develop new knowledge and these information literacy components fall into a no manâs land between the generally accepted roles for librarians and teaching faculty. Shared their observations and insights along with the readings and activities that made up the syllabus for the Learning Community.

2.7 CONCLUSION

From the above review of literature, the following inferences could be drawn :

1. Several studies have been made on the application of Information and Communication Technology (ICT) and Digital Knowledge Management (DKM) in the academic, university, research and corporate sector library and information centers.
2. Highlighted the significance of ICT Knowledge related sources such as e-learning, e-resources, INFONET Consortium visual learning.

3. Identified the importance of Digital Rights Management (DRM), Digital Repository (DR), Electronic Resource Management System (ERMS) and Electronic Information Resources (EIR).
4. Emphasizes the need for Internet and Intranet search facilities, E-mail, Facsimile, the audio-visual aids facilities and Radio Frequency Identification (RFID) technology and Quick Reference code (QR) technologies and also the need of joining in National Knowledge Network (NKN), National Programme on Technology Enhanced Learning (NPTEL).
5. Study Webs of Active-Learning for Young Aspiring Minds (SWAYAM) and National Digital Libraries (NDL) to the University libraries.
6. ICT tools such as Online Public Access Catalogues (OPACs), Circulation Control using Bar-Coding System, Acquisition and Serial Control.
7. Resource Sharing and Networking facilities, Document Delivery Services (DDS) and E-Reference service facilities in view of Electronic Selective Dissemination of Information (ESDI).
8. Attitudes of Library and Information Science (LIS) professionals towards implementation of ICT in library and information centers.
9. Literature reviewed has also identified certain factors such as lack of finance, lack of training etc. which hinders the promotion of ICT in library and information centers.
10. Fair number of intensive studies has been covered in relation to ICT application concepts, services and planning strategies.

However, it is observed that the studies did not emphasis on software packages for library operations, except the SOUL and AUTOLIB. They have also not provided the clear idea about operating system, software and hardware compatibilities required to the present information knowledge management.

Further, it is observed that these studies offer generic trend in different types of libraries in the application of ICT. The status of Deemed University and Central University libraries are not duly covered since the studies on them are not traced in the literature.

Therefore, the present research study fills these gaps and attempts to study the organizational environment changes between the state and deemed university libraries for ICT application based information handling services in and around Chennai.

Chapter III

UNIVERSITY LIBRARY AND INFORMATION CENTRES UNDER SURVEY: THE STATE-OF-THE-ART

3.1 INTRODUCTION

In this chapter an attempt has been made to present an analysis of State-of-the-Art of the University Library and Information Centers under survey. It is to mention that a total number of 24 University Library and Information Centers have been identified and surveyed (Appendix C) in relation to the research theme on "Digital Knowledge Management in the University Library and Information Centers in Chennai (Madras) : An Analytical Study" and for this purpose of description, the libraries have been grouped broadly in three categories namely State, Central and Deemed University Libraries. The list of universities is shown in Table 3.1.

Table 3.1 Universities in Chennai

S.No	Name of the University	Type
1	Indian Maritime University - Chennai	CU
2	IIT Madras	CU
3	Anna University	SU
4	Dr. Ambedkar Law university	SU
5	Tamil Nadu Open University	SU
6	Tamil Nadu Physical Education and Sports University	SU

S.No	Name of the University	Type
7	Tamil Nadu Teachers Education University	SU
8	Tamil Nadu Veterinary and Animal Sciences University	SU
9	The Tamil Nadu Dr. M. G. R. Medical University	SU
10	University of Madras	SU
11	AMET University	DU
12	B. S. Abdur Rahman University	DU
13	Bharat University	DU
14	Chettinad University	DU
15	Dr. M.G.R. Educational and Research Institute	DU
16	Hindustan University	DU
17	Meenakshi Academy of Higher Education and Research	DU
18	Sathyabama University	DU
19	Saveetha University	DU
20	SRM University	DU
21	Vels University	DU
22	VIT University	DU
23	Veltech University	DU
24	St Peters University	DU

It is seen from the Table 3.1 that there are different categories divided into 8 State Universities, 2 Central Universities and 14 Deemed Universities which come into the total of 24 universities.

3.2 STATE-OF-THE ART OF THE STATE UNIVERSITY LIBRARIES

In Chennai there are eight University libraries covering different disciplines. The list of state university libraries are shown in the Table 3.2.

Table 3.2 State Universities – General Information

S.No	University Name	Year of establishment	URL	Subject
1	Anna University	1978	http://www.annauniv.edu	Technology
2	Madras University	1857	http://wwws.unom.ac.in/	General
3	Tamil Nadu Open University	2002	http://www.tnou.ac.in	Distance Education
4	Tamil Nadu Teacher Education University	2008	http://www.tnteu.in/	Education
5	Tamilnadu Dr. Ambedkar Law University	1997	http://www.tndalu.ac.in	Legal Studies
6	Tamilnadu Dr. M.G.R. Medical University	1987	http://www.tnmgrmu.ac.in/	Health Sciences
7	Tamilnadu Physical Education and Sports University	2005	http://www.tnpesu.org	Sports & physical education
8	Tamilnadu Veterinary & Animal Sciences University	1989	http://www.tanuvas.tn.nic.in	Animal Sciences

It is seen from the Table 3.2 that the oldest State University is University of Madras which had been constructed in the year 1857 and the youngest State University is Tamil Nadu Teacher Education University which had been constructed in the year 2008. All the State Universities are administered by the State Government of Tamil Nadu.

The other details such as (i) Library Infrastructure (ii) ICT Facilities (iii) Services, (iv) Reasons for poor digital knowledge management for digital libraries and (v) Attitude towards digital libraries are shown in the ensuing tables as indicated below.

Table 3.3 State Universities - Library Infrastructure

S. No.	University Name	Area Sq. M	Seating capacity	No of books	No of titles	No of print journals
1	Anna University	4200	400	134858	28325	206
2	Madras University	8000	600	526675	42125	400
3	Tamil Nadu Open University	800	130	23721	15400	206
4	Tamil Nadu Teacher Education University	700	125	42001	18510	220
5	Tamilnadu Dr. Ambedkar Law University	1200	120	23308	2750	40
6	Tamilnadu Dr. M.G.R.Medical University	600	125	49350	16450	210

S. No.	University Name	Area Sq. M	Seating capacity	No of books	No of titles	No of print journals
7	Tamilnadu Physical Education and Sports University	500	100	3040	925	34
8	Tamilnadu Veterinary & Animal Sciences University	1150	120	40000	9625	65

The Table 3.3 shows that the state university infrastructure facilities such as areas in sq. mtrs., seating capacities, number of titles, number of books, journals, etc. It is clearly shows that the University of Madras is larger in area as it possesses 8000 sq.metre and the lowest university is Tamilnadu Physical Education and Sports University with 500 sq.meter.

The seating capacity is highest with 600 seats in the University of Madras the seating capacity is lowest in the Tamil Nadu Physical Education and Sports University with just 100 seats. The number of books in the University of Madras is very high with 526675 books whereas in the Tamil Nadu Physical Education and Sports University, the number of books is very low with 3,040 books.

The titles of books in the University of Madras is very high with 42125 titles wherein the titles of books are very low with just 925 in the Tamil Nadu Physical Education and Sports University. The journals that have been printed in the University of Madras is very high with 400 while in the Tamil Nadu Physical Education and Sports University, the titles that have been printed so far is very low with only 34 journals.

Table 3.4 State Universities - ICT Facilities

S.No	University Name	Automation Software Name	E-Journals	E-Books	Digital Library	E-learning Materials	Institutional Repositories
1	Anna University	AUTOLIB	12300	48000	✓	Tele / Video Conferencing	✓
						On-line Databases	
						NPTEL e-Learning Facility	
						Multimedia Resource Service	
2	University of Madras	SOUL	4500	26350	✓	Tele / Video Conferencing	✓
						On-line Databases	
						NPTEL e-Learning Facility	
						Multimedia Resource Service	

S.No	University Name	Automation Software Name	E-Journals	E-Books	Digital Library	E-learning Materials	Institutional Repositories
3	Tamil Nadu Open University	AUTOLIB	206	11500	✓	NKN NDL NPTEL e-Learning Facility Multimedia Resource Service	✓
4	Tamil Nadu Teacher Education University	AUTOLIB	235	2500	✓	DELNET NDL INFLIBNET On-line Databases NPTEL e-Learning Facility Multimedia Resource Service	✓

S.No	University Name	Automation Software Name	E-Journals	E-Books	Digital Library	E-learning Materials	Institutional Repositories
5	Tamilnadu Dr. Ambedkar Law University	KOHA	7032	21	✓	NPTEL e-Learning Facility Multimedia Resource Service DELNET NDL INFLIBNET	✓
6	Tamilnadu Dr. M.G.R. Medical University	IN-HOUSE	6725	325	✓	Tele / Video Conferencing On-line Databases NPTEL e-Learning Facility Multimedia Resource Service	✓

S.No	University Name	Automation Software Name	E-Journals	E-Books	Digital Library	E-learning Materials	Institutional Repositories
7	Tamilnadu Physical Education and Sports University	NIRMALS	7	350	✓	ICU NKN NDL NPTEL e-Learning Facility Multimedia Resource Service	✓
8	Tamilnadu Veterinary & Animal Sciences University	KOHA	2500	250	✓	MALIBNET NKN NDL NPTEL e-Learning Facility	✓

From the Table 3.4, it is seen clearly that the state university libraries, the ICT facilities such as automation software name, E-journals, E-books, Digital library, E-learning materials and institutional repositories are being used for library automation. E-journals are subscribed in major ratios. E-books, Digital library, E-learning materials, and Institutional Repositories are also very widely used in the state university libraries.

Table 3.5 : State Universities - Services

S. No	University Name	Traditional Service				Documentation Service					Computerized Service				
		Circulation	Reservation	ILL	Supply of documents	Indexing/ Abstracting	Biblio graphy	CAS	ESDI	Repro graphy	CD-ROM	Internet	Online Database service	fax	E-mail
1	Anna University	✓	✓	✓	✓	✓	✓	✓	✓	✓	✓	✓	✓	✓	✓
2	Madras University	✓	✓	✓	✓	✓	✓	✓	✓	✓	✓	✓	✓	✓	✓
3	Tamil Nadu Open University	✓	✓	✓	✓	✓	✓	✓	✓	✓	✓	✓	✓	✓	✓
4	Tamil Nadu Teacher Education University	✓	✓	✓	✓	✓	✓	✓	✓	✓	✓	✓	✓	✓	✓
5	Tamilnadu Dr. Ambedkar Law University	✓	✓	✓	✓	✓	✓	✓	✓	✓	✓	✓	✓	✓	✓
6	Tamilnadu Dr. M.G.R.Medical University	✓	✓	✓	✓	✓	✓	✓	✓	✓	✓	✓	✓	✓	✓
7	Tamilnadu Physical Education and Sports University	✓	✓	✓	✓	✓	✓	✓	✓	✓	✓	✓	✓	✓	✓
8	Tamilnadu Veterinary & Animal Sciences University	✓	✓	✓	✓	✓	✓	✓	✓	✓	✓	✓	✓	✓	✓

Table 3.5 shows that there are three kinds of services such as (i) Traditional Services, (ii) Documentation services and (iii) Computerized services have been offered by the state university libraries.

Table 3.6 State Universities - Reasons for Poor Digital Knowledge Management for Digital Libraries

S. No	University Name	Insufficient funds	Inability to absorb recurring costs	Library staff members are not interested in ICT adoption in the library	Lack of adequate trained staff in ICT application	Lack of coordination among the library staff	Lack of Initiative on the part of library professionals	No of support from the Authorities for ICT application in the library	Lack of interest on the part of the readers	Lack of scope for the library professional due to IT applications	The library professionals are not interested in the learning ICT application in the library due to the poor scale of pay for them	Lack of professional recognition by Authority of the library	In accurate Expectations of information communication technology	A fear of modern Information Technology	Lack of Internet access facilities to the users community
1	Anna University	A	A	DA	A	A	A	A	A	DA	DA	A	A	A	A
2	Madras University	A	A	DA	A	A	A	A	A	DA	DA	A	A	A	A
3	Tamil Nadu Open University	A	A	DA	A	A	A	A	A	DA	DA	A	A	A	A
4	Tamil Nadu Teacher Education University	A	A	DA	A	A	DA	A	A	DA	DA	A	A	A	A
5	Tamilnadu Dr. Ambedkar Law University	A	A	DA	A	A	A	A	A	DA	DA	A	A	A	A
6	Tamilnadu Dr. M.G.R.Medical University	A	A	DA	A	A	A	DA	A	DA	DA	A	A	A	A

S. No	University Name	Insufficient funds	Inability to absorb recurring costs	Library staff members are not interested in ICT adoption in the library	Lack of adequate trained staff in ICT application	Lack of coordination among the library staff	Lack of Initiative on the part of library professionals	No of support from the Authorities for ICT application in the library	Lack of interest on the part of the readers	Lack of scope for the library professional due to IT applications	The library professionals are not interested in the learning ICT application in the library due to the poor scale of pay for them	Lack of professional recognition by Authority of the library	In accurate Expectations of information communication technology	A fear of modern Information Technology	Lack of Internet access facilities to the users community
7	Tamilnadu Physical Education and Sports University	A	A	DA	A	A	A	A	A	DA	DA	A	A	A	A
8	Tamilnadu Veterinary & Animal Sciences University	A	A	DA	A	A	A	A	A	DA	DA	A	A	A	A

The Table 3.6 very clearly shows the various reasons for the poor digital knowledge management in the digital libraries of the state universities in and around Chennai City.

Table 3.7 State Universities - Attitude towards Digital Library

S.No	University Name	Improve of the quality of the Library and Information Services(LIS)	Efficiency of the library	Knowledge and expertise	Makes an integration within the organization	essential to improve the communication facilities	Helpful to obtain the right information at the right time in the right place and at the right cost	Status of the library and information centers	Disturb the routine work of the library	Reduces the work load of the library professionals	Takes over the traditional way of information handling in the libraries and information centers	Application will spoil the image of the libraries and information centers
1	Anna University	A	A	A	DA	A	A	A	DA	A	A	DA
2	Madras University	A	A	A	DA	A	A	A	DA	A	A	DA
3	Tamil Nadu Open University	A	A	A	DA	A	A	A	DA	A	A	DA
4	Tamil Nadu Teacher Education University	A	A	A	DA	A	A	A	DA	A	A	DA
5	Tamilnadu Dr. Ambedkar Law University	DA	A	DA	DA	A	A	A	DA	A	A	DA

S.No	**University Name**	**Improve of the quality of the Library and Information Services(LIS)**	**Efficiency of the library**	**Knowledge and expertise**	**Makes an integration within the organization**	**essential to improve the communication facilities**	**Helpful to obtain the right information at the right time in the right place and at the right cost**	**Status of the library and information centers**	**Disturb the routine work of the library**	**Reduces the work load of the library professionals**	**Takes over the traditional way of information handling in the libraries and information centers**	**Application will spoil the image of the libraries and information centers**
6	Tamilnadu Dr. M.G.R.Medical University	A	A	A	DA	A	A	A	DA	A	DA	DA
7	Tamilnadu Physical Education and Sports University	A	A	A	DA	A	DA	A	DA	A	A	DA
8	Tamilnadu Veterinary & Animal Sciences University	A	A	A	DA	A	DA	A	DA	A	A	DA

Table 3.7 shows the attitudes of the state university staff members towards the reluctance of the digital knowledge management in the digital libraries of the State in and around Chennai city.

3.3 STATE-OF-THE ART OF THE DEEMED UNIVERSITY LIBRARIES AND INFORMATIONCENTERS

In Chennai there are Fourteen Deemed Universities covering different disciplines such as Engineering and Technology, Maritime Education, Management Studies, Humanities and Social Sciences etc. Therefore, in the Table 3.8, fourteen libraries have been listed under this category and other details are shown in Tables 3.9 - 3.13.

Table 3.8 Deemed Universities-General Information

S.No	University name	Year of establishment	URL	Subject
1	AMET University	2007	http://www.ametuniv.ac.in	Maritime Science
2	B. S. Abdur Rahman University	2008	http://www.bsauniv.ac.in	Technology
3	Bharat University	2002	http://www.bharathuniv.ac.in	Technology
4	Chettinad University	2008	http://www.chettinadhealthcity.com	Medical
5	Dr. M.G.R. Educational and Research Institute	2008	http://www.hindustanuniv.ac.in	Technology
6	Hindustan University	2003	http://www.drmgrdu.ac.in	Technology
7	Meenakshi Academy of Higher Education and Research	2004	http://www.maher.ac.in	Health Care
8	Sathyabama University	2002	http://www.srmuniv.ac.in	Technology
9	Saveetha University	2001	http://www.sathyabamauniversity.ac.in	Technology
10	SRM University	2005	http://www.saveetha.com	General
11	Vels University	1994	http://www.sriramachandra.edu.in	Technology
12	VIT University	2008	http://www.stpetersuniversity.org	Technology
13	Veltech University	2008	http://www.velsuniv.ac.in	General
14	St Peters University	2008	http://www.veltechuniv.edu.in	Technology

Table 3.9 Deemed University - Library Infrastructure

S. No	**University Name**	**Area** Sq.m	**Seating Capacity**	**No of Books**	**No of Titles**	**No of Print Journals**
1	AMET University	1998	210	64410	20128	144
2	B. S. Abdur Rahman University	3716	240	86087	20996	221
3	Bharat University	2900	200	168273	39868	196
4	Chettinad University	745	45	9000	2236	54
5	Dr. M.G.R. Educational and Research Institute	6650	170	102281	26225	330
6	Hindustan University	6170	325	149577	35492	108
7	Meenakshi Academy of Higher Education and Research	4179	60	33167	7896	149
8	Sathyabama University	13935	425	179212	42669	774
9	Saveetha University	2322	250	106493	28024	417
10	SRM University	3686	125	57705	16487	78
11	Vels University	3716	150	43677	10919	517
12	VIT University	512	75	26963	7095	89
13	Veltech University	2600	295	87521	23441	165
14	St Peters University	1858	225	100549	26460	328

From the Table 3.9, it is seen that the Sathyabama University is the biggest among all the Deemed Universities with 13935 sq.metrs while the VIT is the smallest with just 512 sq.metrs. The seating capacity is very high in Sathyabama University among all the Deemed Universities with 425 seats while the seating capacity is lowest with just 75 seats among those Deemed Universities. The numbers of books are very high with 179212 books in Sathyabama University while the numbers of books are just 26963 in VIT. The numbers of titles are 42669 in Sathyabama University is very high while in VIT the titles are only 7095 which is the lowest. The number of Journals that have been printed in Sathyabama University are 774 which is very high while in VIT the titles are only 89 which is the lowest among all the Deemed Universities.

Table 3.10 Deemed University - ICT Facility

S. No	University Name	Automation Software Name	E-Journals	E-Books	Digital Library	E-Learning Materials	Institutional Repositories
1	AMET University	AUTOLIB	15703	40037	✓	On-line Databases	✓
2	B.S. AbdurRahman University	IN HOUSE	16142	43000	✓	Tele / Video Conferencing On-line Databases NPTEL e-Learning Facility Multimedia Resource Service	✓
3	Bharat University	AUTOLIB	2433	25000	✓	NDL DELNET HELNET NKN NPTEL e-Learning Facility Multimedia Resource Service	✓
4	Chettinad University	AUTOLIB	865	2750	✓	NDL DELNET HELNET NKN NPTEL e-Learning Facility Multimedia Resource Service	✓

S. No	University Name	Automation Software Name	E-Journals	E-Books	Digital Library	E-Learning Materials	Institutional Repositories
5	Dr. M.G.R. Educational and Research Institute	LIBSYS	3245	32416	✓	Tele / Video Conferencing On-line Databases NPTEL e-Learning Facility Multimedia Resource Service	✓
6	Hindustan University	LIBSYS	35812	105250	✓	Tele / Video Conferencing NPTEL e-Learning Facility On-line Databases Multimedia Resource Service	✓
7	Meenakshi Academy of Higher Education and Research	EASY-LIB	1561	2470	✓	On-line Databases NPTEL e-Learning Facility	✓
8	Sathyabama University	AUTOLIB	42300	58000	✓	Tele / Video Conferencing On-line Databases NPTEL e-Learning Facility Multimedia Resource Service	✓
9	Saveetha University	AUTOLIB	3147	64544	✓	Tele / Video C Multimedia Resource Service On-line Databases	✓

S. No	University Name	Automation Software Name	E-Journals	E-Books	Digital Library	E-Learning Materials	Institutional Repositories
10	SRM University	AUTOLIB	6750	1837	✓	On-line Databases NPTEL e-Learning Facility	✓
11	Vels University	IN-HOUSE	2000	8500	✓	Tele / Video Conferencing On-line Databases NPTEL e-Learning Facility Multimedia Resource Service	✓
12	VIT University	AUTOLIB	232	3860	✓	NPTEL e-Learning Facility	✓
13	Veltech University	LIBGENIE	17717	108438	✓	Tele / Video Conferencing On-line Databases NPTEL e-Learning Facility Multimedia Resource Service	✓
14	St Peters University	NIRMALS	3138	45000	✓	Tele / Video Conferencing NPTEL e-Learning Facility Multimedia Resource Service	✓

Table 3.11 Deemed University - Services

S. No	University Name	Traditional Service				Documentation Service					Computerized Service				
		Circulation	Reservation	ILL	Supply of Documents / Articles	Indexing/Abstracting	Bibliography	CAS	ESDI	Reprography	CD-ROM	Internet	Online Database service	FAX	E-mail
1	AMET University	✓	✓	✓	✓	-	✓	✓	-	✓	✓	✓	✓	✓	✓
2	B.S. Abdur Rahman University	✓	✓	✓	✓	✓	✓	✓	✓	✓	✓	✓	✓	✓	✓
3	Bharat University	✓	✓	✓	✓	✓	✓	✓	✓	✓	✓	✓	✓	✓	✓
4	Chettinad University	✓	✓	✓	✓	✓	✓	✓	✓	✓	✓	✓	✓	✓	✓
5	Dr. M.G.R. Educational and Research Institute	✓	✓	✓	✓	✓	✓	✓	✓	✓	✓	✓	✓	✓	✓
6	Hindustan University	✓	✓	✓	✓	✓	✓	✓	✓	✓	✓	✓	✓	✓	✓
7	Meenakshi Academy of Higher Education and Research	✓	✓	✓	✓	✓	✓	✓	-	✓	✓	✓	✓	✓	✓

S. No	University Name	Traditional Service				Documentation Service					Computerized Service				
		Circulation	**Reservation**	**ILL**	**Supply of Documents / Articles**	**Indexing/Abstracting**	**Bibliography**	**CAS**	**ESDI**	**Reprography**	**CD-ROM**	**Internet**	**Online Database service**	**FAX**	**E-mail**
8	Sathyabama University	✓	✓	✓	✓	✓	✓	✓	-	✓	✓	✓	✓	✓	✓
9	Saveetha University	✓	✓	✓	✓	✓	✓	✓	✓	✓	✓	✓	✓	✓	✓
10	SRM University	✓	✓	✓	✓	-	✓	✓	-	✓	✓	✓	✓	✓	✓
11	Vels University	✓	✓	✓	✓	✓	✓	✓	-	✓	✓	✓	✓	✓	✓
12	VIT University	✓	✓	✓	✓	-	✓	✓	-	✓	✓	✓	✓	✓	✓
13	Veltech University	✓	✓	✓	✓	✓	✓	✓	✓	✓	✓	✓	✓	✓	✓
14	St Peters University	✓	✓	✓	✓	✓	✓	✓	✓	✓	✓	✓	✓	✓	✓

From the Table 3.11, it is seen that three types services such as (a) Traditional Services, (b) Documentation Services and (c) Computerized Services are being offered in the Deemed University and Information Centers and around Chennai City.

Table 3.12 Deemed University - Reasons for Poor Digital Knowledge Management for Digital Libraries

S.No	University Name	Insufficient funds	Inability to absorb recurring costs	Library staff members are not interested in ICT adoption in the library	Lack of adequate trained staff in ICT application	Lack of coordination among the library staff	Lack of Initiative on the part of library professionals	No of support from the Authorities for ICT application in the library	Lack of interest on the part of the readers	Lack of scope for the library professional due to ICT applications	The library professionals are not interested in the learning ICT application in the library due to the poor scale of pay for them	Lack of professional recognition by Authority of the library	In accurate Expectations of information communication technology	A fear of modern Information communication Technology	Lack of Internet access facilities to the users community
1	AMET University	A	A	DA	A	A	A	A	A	DA	DA	A	A	A	A
2	B. S. Abdur Rahman University	A	A	DA	A	A	A	A	A	DA	DA	A	A	DA	A
3	Bharat University	A	A	DA	A	DA	A	A	DA	DA	DA	A	A	A	A
4	Chettinad University	A	A	DA	A	DA	A	A	A	DA	DA	A	A	DA	A

S.No	University Name	Insufficient funds	Inability to absorb recurring costs	Library staff members are not interested in ICT adoption in the library	Lack of adequate trained staff in ICT application	Lack of coordination among the library staff	Lack of Initiative on the part of library professionals	No of support from the Authorities for ICT application in the library	Lack of interest on the part of the readers	Lack of scope for the library professional due to ICT applications	The library professionals are not interested in the learning ICT application in the library due to the poor scale of pay for them	Lack of professional recognition by Authority of the library	In accurate Expectations of information communication technology	A fear of modern Information communication Technology	Lack of Internet access facilities to the users community
5	Dr. M.G.R. Educational and Research Institute	A	A	DA	A	A	A	A	A	DA	DA	A	A	A	A
6	Hindustan University	A	A	DA	A	A	DA	A	A	DA	DA	A	A	A	A
7	Meenakshi Academy of Higher Education and Research	A	A	DA	A	A	A	DA	A	DA	DA	A	A	A	A
8	Sathyabama University	A	A	DA	A	A	A	A	A	DA	DA	A	A	A	A

S.No	University Name	Insufficient funds	Inability to absorb recurring costs	Library staff members are not interested in ICT adoption in the library	Lack of adequate trained staff in ICT application	Lack of coordination among the library staff	Lack of Initiative on the part of library professionals	No of support from the Authorities for ICT application in the library	Lack of interest on the part of the readers	Lack of scope for the library professional due to ICT applications	The library professionals are not interested in the learning ICT application in the library due to the poor scale of pay for them	Lack of professional recognition by Authority of the library	In accurate Expectations of information communication techology	A fear of modern Information communication Technology	Lack of Internet access facilities to the users community
9	Saveetha University	A	A	DA	A	A	A	A	A	DA	DA	A	A	A	A
10	SRM University	A	A	DA	A	A	DA	A	A	DA	DA	A	A	DA	A
11	Vels University	A	A	DA	A	A	A	A	A	DA	DA	A	DA	A	A
12	VIT University	A	A	DA	A	A	DA	A	A	DA	DA	A	A	DA	A
13	Veltech University	A	A	DA	A	A	A	A	A	DA	DA	A	A	A	A
14	St Peters University	A	A	DA	A	A	A	A	A	DA	DA	A	A	A	A

From the Table 3.12, it is seen the various reasons that have paved the ways for the poor Digital Knowledge Management in the deemed university and information centers in and around Chennai. Most of the deemed university libraries will very soon take the appropriate methods for removing the prevailing state of the poor Digital Knowledge Management in the ensuing digital era.

Table 3.13 Deemed University-Attitude towards Digital Library

S.No	University Name	Improve of the quality of the Library and Information Services(LIS)	Efficiency of the library	Knowledge and expertise	Makes an integration within the organization	Essential to improve the communication facilities	Helpful to obtain the right information at the right time in the right place and at the right cost	Status of the library and information centers	Disturb the routine work of the library	Reduces the work load of the library professionals	Takes over the traditional way of information handling in the libraries and information centers	Application will spoil the image of the libraries and information centers
1	AMET University	A	A	A	DA	A	A	A	DA	A	A	DA
2	B. S. Abdur Rahman University	A	A	A	DA	A	A	A	DA	A	A	DA
3	Bharat University	A	A	A	DA	A	DA	A	DA	A	DA	DA
4	Chettinad University	A	A	A	DA	A	A	A	DA	A	A	DA
5	Dr. M.G.R. Educational and Research Institute	A	A	DA	DA	A	A	A	DA	A	A	DA
6	Hindustan University	A	A	A	DA	A	A	A	DA	A	A	DA

S.No	University Name	Improve of the quality of the Library and Information Services(LIS)	Efficiency of the library	Knowledge and expertise	Makes an integration within the organization	Essential to improve the communication facilities	Helpful to obtain the right information at the right time in the right place and at the right cost	Status of the library and information centers	Disturb the routine work of the library	Reduces the work load of the library professionals	Takes over the traditional way of information handling in the libraries and information centers	Application will spoil the image of the libraries and information centers
7	Meenakshi Academy of Higher Education & Research	A	A	DA	DA	A	A	A	DA	A	A	DA
8	Sathyabama University	A	A	A	DA	A	A	A	DA	A	A	DA
9	Saveetha University	A	A	A	DA	A	DA	A	DA	A	DA	DA
10	SRM University	A	DA	A	DA	A	A	A	DA	A	DA	DA
11	Vels University	A	A	A	DA	A	A	A	DA	A	A	DA
12	VIT University	A	A	DA	DA	A	DA	A	DA	A	DA	DA
13	Veltech University	A	A	A	DA	A	A	A	DA	A	A	DA
14	St Peters University	A	A	A	DA	A	A	A	DA	A	A	DA

From the Table 3.13, it is seen the attitude of the knowledge management staff members that do not make much progress of the digital knowledge management in the deemed university library and information centers.

3.4 STATE-OF-THE ART OF THE CENTRAL UNIVERSITIES

Though there are two central Universities libraries and Information Centers are available in and around Chennai, only one library has introduced the ICT applications. Hence, the details pertaining to those two central Universities libraries and Information Centers are given in Table 3.14. The two libraries have been listed under this category and other details are shown in Tables 3.15 - 3.13.

Table 3.14 Central University - General Information

S. No.	University Name	Year of establishment	URL	Subject
1	Indian Maritime University	1985	http://www.imu.edu.in/	Maritime
2	Indian Institute of Technology	1959	https://www.iitm.ac.in/	Technology

It is seen from the Table 3.14 that the Indian Institute of Technology (IIT) is older as it had been constructed in the year 1959 while the Indian Maritime University (IMU) had been constructed in the year 1985.

Table 3.15 Central University - Library Infrastructure

S. No	University Name	Area Sq.m	Seating Capacity	No of Books	No of Titles	No of Print Journals
1	Indian Maritime University	950	80	22426	3780	119
2	Indian Institute of Technology	1100	1050	116000	43122	240

From the Table 3.15, it is seen that the Indian Institute of Technology (IIT) is very big as it has been constructed in the 1100 sq.mtrs. while the Indian Maritime University (IMU) is constructed in just 950 sq.mtrs. The seating capacity in IIT is very high with 1050 seats while the IMU is very low with just 80 seats only.

The number of books in IIT library is vast with 116000 books while the IMU library is having only 22426 books. The number of titles in the IIT Library is very high with 43122 titles while in the IMU library, the titles are 3780 only. The number of journals that have been printed so far in IIT Library are 240 whereas in IMU Library, the journals that have been printed so far are just 119 only.

Table 3.16 Central University - ICT Facility

S.No	University Name	Automation Software Name	E-Journals	E-Books	Digital Library	E-Learning Materials	Institutional Repositories
1	Indian Maritime University	KOHA	3650	876	✓	NPTEL e-Learning Facility Multimedia Resource Service	✓
2	Indian Institute of Technology	LIBSYS	1232	167	✓	Tele / Video Conferencing On-line Databases NPTEL e-Learning Facility Multimedia Resource Service	✓

From the Table 3.16, it is seen that the Automation Software, E-Journals, E-Books, Digital Library, E-Learning materials and Institutional Repositories are being used both in the Indian Institute of Technology (IIT) and in the Indian Maritime University (IMU).

Table 3.17 Central University - Services

	Des cription	Traditional Service				Documentation Service					Computerised Service				
S.No	**University Name**	**Circulation**	**Reservation**	**ILL**	**Supply of Documents / Articles**	**Indexing / Abstracting**	**Bibliography**	**CAS**	**E-SDI**	**Reprography**	**CD-ROM**	**Internet**	**Online Database Service**	**FAx**	**E-mail**
1	Indian Maritime Univer sity	✓	✓	✓	✓	✓	✓	✓	✓	✓	✓	✓	✓	✓	✓
2	Indian Institute of Tech nology	✓	✓	✓	✓	✓	✓	✓	✓	✓	✓	✓	✓	✓	✓

From the Table 3.17, it is seen that the three types of services namely the Traditional Service, Documentation Service and Computerized Services are being offered to the Digital and Traditional Library Users in both the Indian Institute of Technology (IIT) and in the Indian Maritime University) IMU).

Table 3.18 Central University - Reasons for Poor Digital Knowledge Management for Digital Librarians

S.No	University Name	Insufficient funds	Inability to absorb recurring costs	Library staff members are not interested in ICT adoption in the library	Lack of adequate trained staff in ICT application	Lack of coordination among the library staff	Lack of Initiative on the part of library professionals	No of support from the Authorities for ICT application in the library	Lack of interest on the part of the readers	Lack of scope for the library professional due to ICT applications	The library professionals are not interested in the learning ICT application in the library due to the poor scale of pay for them	Lack of professional recognition by Authority of the library	In accurate Expectations of information communication technology	A fear of modern Information communication Technology	Lack of Internet access facilities to the users community
1	Indian Mari time Univer sity-	A	A	DA	A	A	A	A	A	DA	DA	A	A	A	A
2	Indian Inst itute of Techno logy	A	A	DA	A	A	A	A	A	DA	DA	A	A	A	A

Table 3.18 shows the reasons that exist behind the poor knowledge of digital knowledge on the parts of the digital Libraries in the Central Universities like Indian Maritime University (IMU).

Table 3.19 Central University - Attitude towards Digital Library

S.No	University Name	Improve of the quality of the Library and Information Services(LIS)	Efficiency of the library	Knowledge and expertise	Makes an integration within the organization	Essential to improve the communication facilities	Helpful to obtain the right information at the right time in the right place and at the right cost	Status of the library and information centers	Disturb the routine work of the library	Reduces the work load of the library professionals	Takes over the traditional way of information handling in the libraries and information centers	Application will spoil the image of the libraries and information centers
1	Indian Mari time Univer sity-	A	DA	A	A	A	A	A	DA	A	A	A
2	Indian Insti tute of Techno logy	A	A	DA	DA	A	A	A	DA	A	DA	DA

Table 3.19 shows the attitudes of the digital library users towards utilizing the digital knowledge management by the digital and traditional library users in both the digital and traditional libraries in the Central Universities like the Indian Institute of Technology (IIT) and Indian Maritime University (IMU).

3.5 CONCLUSION

From the above presentation of the state-of-the-art of the University Library and Information Centers, the following remarks are offered :

i. There are twenty four universities in and around Chennai which applied ICT applications in relation to Digital Knowledge Management in the University Library and Information Centers.

ii. Out of these twenty four university libraries, eight represents State University, two represents Central University Library and Information Centers and fourteen Deemed University library and information centers.

iii. The State University Libraries are grouped into eight divisions namely :

    a. Anna University
    b. Dr. Ambedkar Law University
    c. Tamil Nadu Open University
    d. Tamil Nadu Physical Education and Sports University
    e. Tamil Nadu Teachers Education University
    f. Tamil Nadu Veterinary and Animal Sciences University
    g. The Tamil Nadu Dr. M.G.R. Medical University
    h. University of Madras

iv. The Central University Library category are grouped into two divisions namely :

    a. Indian Maritime University-Chennai Campus
    b. Indian Institute of Technology (IIT)

v. The Deemed University Library category are grouped into fourteen divisions namely :

    a. AMET University
    b. B.S Abdur Rahman University

c. Bharat University
d. Chettinad University
e. Dr. M.G.R. Educational and Research Institute
f. Hindustan University
g. Meenakshi Academy of Higher Education and Research
h. Sathyabama University
i. Saveetha University
j. SRM University
k. St Peters University
l. Vels University
m. VIT University
n. Veltech University

vi. The application of ICT is seen since 1990s in the libraries under study.

vii. The design and development of webOPACs is the major area in all libraries under survey.

viii. Most of the library and information centers used commercial software packages like Libsys, Autolib, SOUL etc. for automation purposes.

ix. In most of the University Library and Information Centers joined with resource sharing and networks namely MALIBNET, INFLIBNET, DELNET, ERNET, NKN, NDL, etc.

x. The provision of database services are seen mostly in all university library and information centers.

xi. The provision of Internet and E-Mail services are attached to all the University Library and Information Centers

xii. The application of ICT is seen in all the University Library and Information Centers under study.

xiii. A majority of libraries have acquired the facilities like reprographic, Fax, Printers, Scanners, Audio-Visual Aids and most of the libraries have the digital resources.

In the next chapter, a detailed analysis and interpretation of the data on these library and information centers are presented.

Chapter IV

MATERIALS & METHODS

4.1 INTRODUCTION

In the previous chapter, the State-of-art-of-the University Library and Information Centers in and around Chennai that have the Digital Knowledge Management (DRM) and Information and Communication Technology (ICT) has been presented. In this chapter, analysis and interpretation of data collected from these centers through questionnaire (Appendix-A & B) as portraited in chapter one under sections (1.9 to 1.12) relation to the concepts on Materials and Methods.The Materials such as tools for data collection, pilot study, development of final questionnaire and sampling. The methods in terms of advanced SPSS tools used for analysis. The Analysis has been presented in two ways:

i. Descriptive analysis
ii. Differential analysis

Descriptive analysis of data is in terms of frequency distribution distributed on percentage. Differential analysis is in terms of advanced SPSS statistical techniques such as, Mean, Median, Mode, Standard Deviation, Clustering Analysis and Proximity Matrix. Besides presenting the data in a tabular form, graphical presentation such as pie chart, bar diagram and linear graph have also been used. The results of the study as identified in the following ways and means.

4.2 SAMPLE SIZE

The questionnaire was administrated among 2400 faculty and research scholars of 24 universities in Chennai. Out of which 2057 have responded and the response rate works out to 85.71%. The Table 4.1 presents the data pertaining to the distribution of questionnaire responses received from the sample.

Table 4.1 Distribution of Questionnaire

S. No	Description	No. of Universities	Questionnaire distributed	Responses received	Percentage
1	Central University	2	200	192	96.00
2	State University	8	800	661	84.84
3	Deemed University	14	1400	1204	86.00
	Total	24	2400	2057	85.71

Response rate = 85.71%

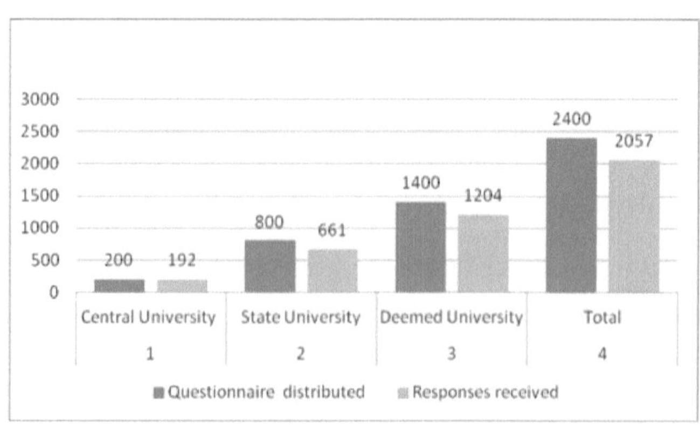

Figure 4.1 Distribution of Questionnaire

Table 4.1 shows the number of questionnaires distributed and the responses received from the participants. It is evident that the respondents from 2 Central university have responded with 96%, followed by 14 Deemed Universities and 8 state universities with 86% and 84.84% respectively. Out of 2400 questionnaires distributed, 2057 questionnaires were received 85.71% totally.

4.2.1 Demographic Details of Respondents

The demographic details of the respondents were shown in Table 4.2.

From the ***Table 4.2,*** it can be inferred that the respondents population is higher from deemed universities, followed by state and central universities. Respondents were classified in to two main categories namely Research scholars (70.1%) and Faculty members (29.9%). Gender wise classification indicates that male participants cater to 68.5% and female participants 31.5%.

Table 4.2 Demographic details of respondents

S.No	Description	Total	Percentage
	Type of University		
1	Central	192	9.3
2	State	661	32.1
3	Deemed	1204	58.5
	Category		
1	Research Scholars	1442	70.1
2	Faculty Members	615	29.9
	Gender		
1	Male	1409	68.5
2	Female	648	31.5
	Overall		
	Total	2057	100.0

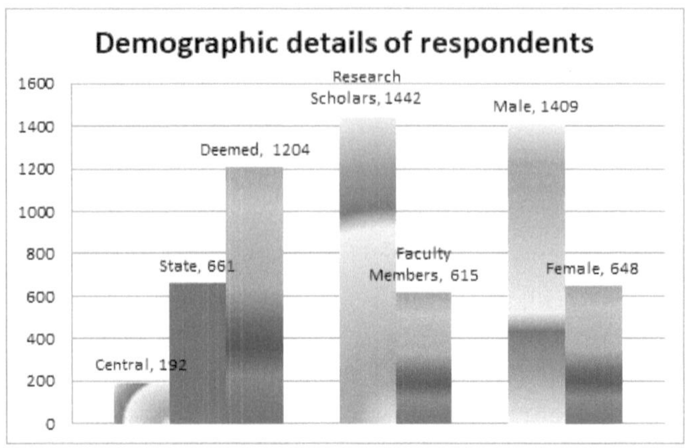

Figure 4.2 Demographic details of respondents

4.3 DIGITAL KNOWLEDGE MANAGEMENT

Digital Knowledge Management has been ascertained based on

- User Expectation
- Essentiality of the Digital knowledge sources and services
- Opinion on available Digital Knowledge Sources and Services.
- Limitations of Digital Knowledge Sources and Services.

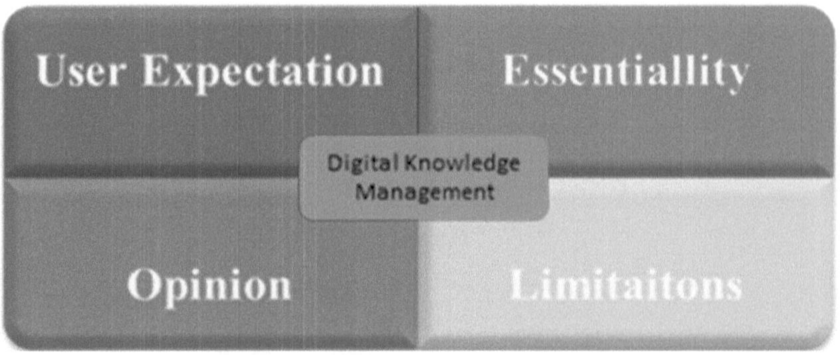

Figure 4.3 Digital Knowledge Management - Concepts

4.4 USER EXPECTATION ON DIGITAL KNOWLEDGE SOURCES AND SERVICES

4.4.1 Visit to Digital Knowledge Resource Centre

Table 4.3 shows the frequency of the users visit to Digital Knowledge Resource Centers. Frequency of visit to Digital Knowledge Resource Centre is estimated in 5 different categories namely daily, once in two days, once in a week, once in fifteen days and once in a month.

Table 4.3 Visit to Digital Knowledge Resource Center

S.No	Time	Frequency	Percentage	Cumulative Percentage
1	Daily	1260	61.3	61.3
2	Once in two days	185	9.0	70.2
3	Once in a week	546	26.5	96.8
4	Once in fifteen days	55	2.7	99.5
5	Once in a month	11	.5	100.0
	Total	2057	100.0	
	Mean	1.72		
	Standard deviation	0.978		
	Median	1.00		
	Mode	1		

Figure 4.4 Visit to Digital Knowledge Resource Centre

It can be inferred from ***Table 4.3 and Figure 4.3,*** that around 61.3% of users are visiting Digital Knowledge Resource Centers daily, followed by once in a week and once in two days. Only few users have indicated that they visit resource centers once in a month. This shows that users from all universities are dependent on the Digital Knowledge Resource centers for their academic needs often.

Table 4.4 shows the frequency of the users' visit against the type of university the respondents belong to. Frequency of visit to Digital KnowledgeResourceCentreisestimatedin5differentcategoriesnamely daily, once in two days, once in a week, once in fifteen days and once in month.

Table 4.4 Visit to Digital Knowledge Resource center Vs Type of University

S. No	Time	Central University		State University		Deemed University		Total	
1	Daily	11	.5%	479	23.3%	770	37.4%	1260	61.3%
2	Once in two days	56	2.7%	30	1.5%	99	4.8%	185	9.0%
3	Once in a week	104	5.1%	138	6.7%	304	14.8%	546	26.5%
4	Once in fifteen days	20	1.0%	10	.5%	25	1.2%	55	2.7%
5	Once in a month	1	.0%	4	.2%	6	.3%	11	.5%
Total		192	9.3%	661	32.1%	1204	58.5%	2057	100.0%

It can be inferred from Table 4.4 and Figure 4.4, that out of 61.3% of users who are visiting Digital Knowledge Resource Centers daily, 37.4% belong to Deemed University followed by 23.3% from State University and 0.5% from Central University. For all categories of frequencies, users from deemed universities are utilizing or visiting Digital Knowledge Resource Centre more than other type of universities comparatively.

Table 4.5 shows gender wise visit to Digital Knowledge Resource centre, against the frequency of visit estimated in 5 different categories namely daily, once in two days, once in a week, once in fifteen days and once in a month.

Table 4.5 Visit to Digital Knowledge Resource Centre Vs Gender

S.No	Time	Male		Female		Total	
1	Daily	884	43.0%	376	18.3%	1260	61.3%
2	Once in two days	137	6.7%	48	2.3%	185	9.0%
3	Once in a week	345	16.8%	201	9.8%	546	26.5%
4	Once in fifteen days	36	1.8%	19	.9%	55	2.7%
5	Once in a month	7	.3%	4	.2%	11	.5%
Total		192	1409	68.5%	648	31.5%	100.0%

From *Table 4.5*, out of 61.3% of users who visit daily 43% are male respondents and 18.3% are female respondents. From the overall gender distribution and usage pattern male respondents utilize more effectively than female respondents for all categories of frequency of visit. It can be inferred that respondents ratio and usage of resources should be motivated among female respondents to bring down the difference between population.

Table 4.6 shows two different type of users categorized with their designation namely Research scholars and faculty members, and their frequency of visit to Digital Knowledge Resource center, estimated in 5 different categories namely daily, once in two days, once in a week, once in fifteen days and once in month.

Table 4.6 Visit to Digital Knowledge Resource Centre Vs Designation

S.No	Time	Research Scholars		Faculty Members		Total	
1	Daily	859	41.8%	401	19.5%	1260	61.3%
2	Once in two days	135	6.6%	50	2.4%	185	9.0%
3	Once in week	404	19.6%	142	6.9%	546	26.5%

S.No	Time	Research Scholars		Faculty Members		Total	
4	Once in fifteen days	35	1.7%	20	1.0%	55	2.7%
5	Once in a month	9	.4%	2	.1%	11	.5%
Total		1442	70.1%	615	29.9%	2057	100.0%

From ***Table 4.6,*** out of 61.3% of users who visit daily 41.8% are research scholars and 19.5% are faculty members according to their designation. From the overall gender distribution and usage pattern male respondents utilize more effectively than female respondents for all categories of frequency of visit. It can be inferred that respondents ratio and usage of resources should be motivated among female respondents to bring down the difference between populations.

Table 4.7 Visit to Digital Knowledge Resource Centre

S.No	Description	Mean	Std.	Median	Verbal scale
	Type of University				
1	Central	2.71	.751	3.00	Once in a week
2	State	1.53	.912	1.00	Daily
3	Deemed	1.67	.955	1.00	Daily
	Category				
1	Research Scholars	1.75	.984	1.00	Daily
2	Faculty Members	1.65	.961	1.00	Daily
	Gender				
1	Male	1.68	.959	1.00	Daily
2	Female	1.81	1.014	1.00	Daily
	Overall				
	Total	1.72	.978	1.00	Daily

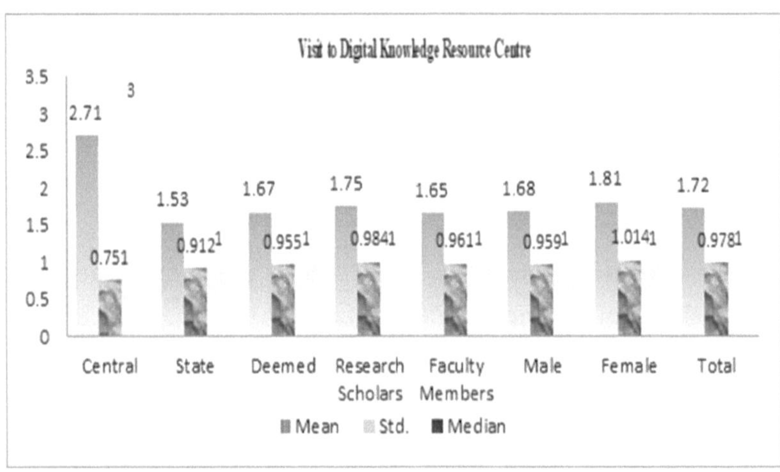

Figure 4.5 Visit to Digital Knowledge Resource Centre Vs categories of respondents

From ***Table 4.7 and Figure 4.4,*** we can infer that all the categories of respondents visit library daily except centrally owned universities. Most of the Central Universities have Wi-Fi enabled campus with full access to digital resources and this facilitates the users without visiting the center personally.

4.4.2 Convenience of Working Hours

Digital Knowledge Centers in different universities has different access policies and timings but the convenience of users was enquired as "Yes" or "No".

Table 4.8 Working hours of the Digital Knowledge Centers

S.No	Description	Frequency	Percentage	Cumulative Percentage
1	Convenient	472	22.9%	22.9%
2	Inconvenient	1585	77.1%	100.0%
	Total	2057	100%	

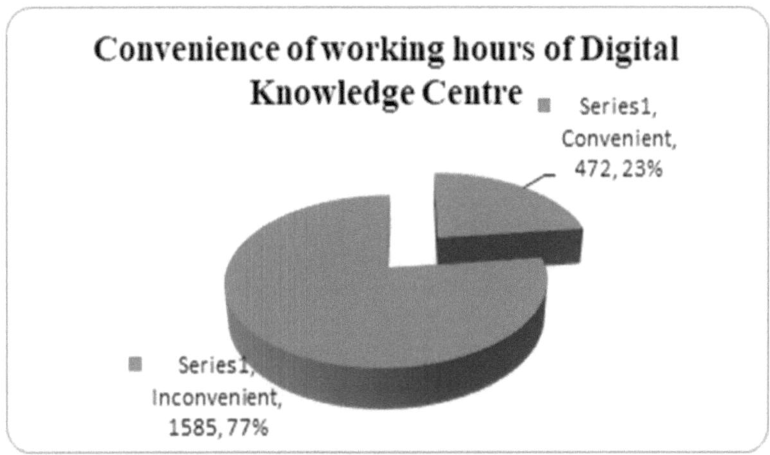

Figure 4.6 Convenience of working hours of Digital Knowledge Resource Centre

From ***Table 4.8 and Figure 4.5*** respondents have indicated their opinion on access or working hours of Digital Knowledge Centres in different universities. More than three fourth (77%) of the respondents have indicated that the working hours was not convenient and this indicates that it requires changes in policy of working hours.

Table 4.9 Working hours of the Digital Knowledge Centers Vs Type of University

S.No	Type of University	Convenient		Inconvenient		Total	
1	Central	109	5.3%	83	4.0%	192	9.3%
2	State	78	3.8%	583	28.3%	661	32.1%
3	Deemed	285	13.9%	919	44.7%	1204	58.5%
	Total	472	22.9%	1585	77.1%	2057	100.0%

From Table 4.9 most of the respondents from all type of universities invariably have indicated that the working hours was inconvenient.

Table 4.10 Working hours of the Digital Knowledge Centers Vs Category

S.No	Type of User Category	Convenient		Inconvenient		Total	
1	Research Scholars	343	16.7%	1099	53.4%	1442	70.1%
2	Faculty Members	129	6.3%	486	23.6%	615	29.9%
	Total	472	22.9%	1585	77.1%	2057	100.0%

Faculty (23.6%) and research scholars (53.4%) have also indicated that the working hours were not convenient for the users to access.

Table 4.11 Working hours of the Digital Knowledge Centers Vs Gender

S.No	Type of Gender	Convenient		Inconvenient		Total	
1	Male	296	14.4%	1113	54.1%	1409	68.5%
2	Female	176	8.6%	472	22.9%	648	31.5%
	Total	472	22.9%	1585	77.1%	2057	100.0%

Respondents have indicated that the timings of were inconvenient for them without gender bias. Male respondents (54.1%) and female respondents (22.9%) totaling to 77.7% of respondents were not satisfied with the working hours.

Table 4.12 : Working hours of the Digital Knowledge Centers

S.No	Description	Mean	Std.	Median	Verbal scale
	Type of University				
1	Central	1.43	.497	1.00	Convenient
2	State	1.88	.323	2.00	Inconvenient
3	Deemed	1.76	.425	2.00	Inconvenient
	Category				
1	Research Scholars	1.76	.426	2.00	Inconvenient

S.No	Description	Mean	Std.	Median	Verbal scale
2	Faculty Members	1.79	.407	2.00	Inconvenient
		Gender			
1	Male	1.79	.408	2.00	Inconvenient
2	Female	1.73	.445	2.00	Inconvenient
		Overall			
	Total	1.77	.421	2.00	Inconvenient

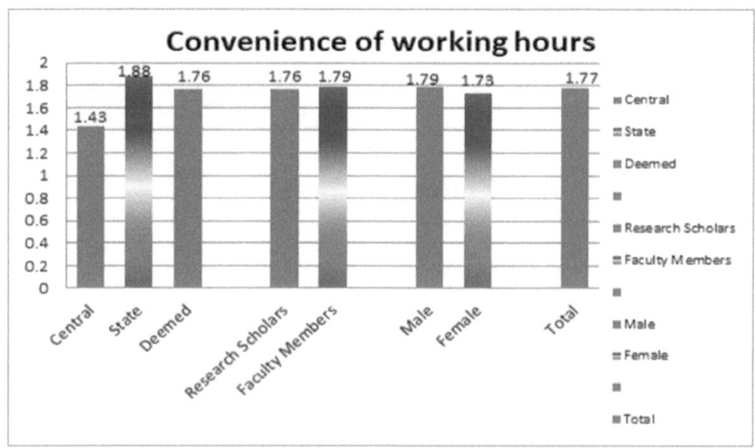

Figure 4.7 Convenience of working hours

Respondents have indicated that the timings of were inconvenient for them without gender bias. Male respondents (54.1%) and female respondents (22.9%) were not satisfied with the working hours.

4.4.3 Convenient Timings

Working hours specifically on working days and holidays were differentiated and the opinion from respondents were received on four different sessions namely "morning session", "noon session", "evening session" and "late night session". The same has been indicated with percentage and the rank.

Table 4.13 Convenient Timings – On Working Days and Holidays

S.No	Convenient Time	Working days		Rank	Holidays		Rank
1	Morning session	615	29.9	2	290	14.1	3
2	Noon session	1097	53.3	1	783	38.1	1
3	Evening session	338	16.4	3	701	34.1	2
4	Late night session	7	.3	4	283	13.8	4
	Total	2057	100.0		2057	100.0	

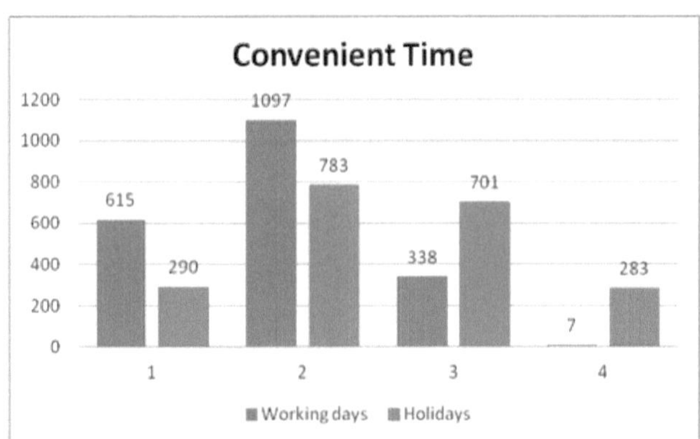

Figure 4.8 Convenient working hours

From ***Table 4.13 and Figure 4.7,*** it can be inferred that noon session was more preferred than other sessions both on working and holidays. Morning session was preferred on working days and evening session on holidays was given second preference. Working hours specifically on working days and holidays were differentiated and the opinion from respondents were received on four different sessions namely "morning session", "noon session", "evening session" and "late night session". The same has been indicated with percentage and the rank.

Table 4.14 Convenient Working Hours – On Working days and Holidays Vs Type of University

S. No.	Time	Working Days								Holidays							
		Central University		State University		Deemed University		Total		Central University		State University		Deemed University		Total	
1	Morning session	166	8.1%	114	5.5%	335	16.3%	615	29.9%	30	1.5%	95	4.6%	165	8.0%	290	14.1%
2	Noon session	14	.7%	398	19.3%	685	33.3%	1097	53.3%	74	3.6%	250	12.2%	459	22.3%	783	38.1%
3	Evening session	5	.2%	149	7.2%	184	8.9%	338	16.4%	63	3.1%	224	10.9%	414	20.1%	701	34.1%
4	Late night session	7	.3%	0	.0%	0	.0%	7	.3%	25	1.2%	92	4.5%	166	8.1%	283	13.8%
	Total	192	9.3%	661	32.1%	1204	58.5%	2057	100.0%	192	9.3%	661	32.1%	1204	58.5%	2057	100.0%

Table 4.14 shows that the noon session followed by evening session was preferred by the respondents from State Universities. The order of preference was indicated as noon session followed by morning session which varies with respondents from Deemed University, whereas morning session was preferred by respondents from Central Universities.

On holidays all the respondents unanimously have indicated that noon session followed by evening session was preferred. Late night sessions were equally preferred on holidays.

Table 4.15 Convenient Working Hours – On Working days and Holidays Vs Category

S.No	Time	Working Days						Holidays					
		Research Scholars		Faculty Members		Total		Research Scholars		Faculty Members		Total	
1	Morning session	444	21.6%	171	8.3%	615	29.9%	199	9.7%	91	4.4%	290	14.1%
2	Noon session	762	37.0%	335	16.3%	1097	53.3%	542	26.3%	241	11.7%	783	38.1%
3	Evening session	231	11.2%	107	5.2%	338	16.4%	490	23.8%	211	10.3%	701	34.1%
4	Late night session	5	.2%	2	.1%	7	.3%	211	10.3%	72	3.5%	283	13.8%
	Total	1442	70.1%	615	29.9%	2057	100.0%	1442	70.1%	615	29.9%	2057	100.0%

Table 4.15 shows that both the categories namely research scholars and faculty members prefer the noon session followed by evening session on working days. On holidays, the order of preference was indicated as noon session followed by evening and late night session for research scholars and noon session followed by evening and morning sessions for faculty members. On the whole late night sessions are kept as last resort on working days.

Table 4.16 Convenient Working Hours – On Working days and Holidays Vs Gender

S.No	Time	Working Days						Holidays					
		Male		Female		Total		Male		Female		Total	
1	Morning session	354	17.2%	261	12.7%	615	29.9%	199	9.7%	91	4.4%	290	14.1%
2	Noon session	815	39.6%	282	13.7%	1097	53.3%	530	25.8%	253	12.3%	783	38.1%
3	Evening session	236	11.5%	102	5.0%	338	16.4%	483	23.5%	218	10.6%	701	34.1%
4	Late night session	4	.2%	3	.1%	7	.3%	197	9.6%	86	4.2%	283	13.8%
	Total	1409	68.5%	648	31.5%	2057	100.0%	1409	68.5%	648	31.5%	2057	100.0%

Both male and female respondents invariably prefer noon session followed by morning session and evening session on working days and holidays but equal importance was given to late night sessions also on holidays alone. There is no significant difference in opinion among respondents on the basis of gender.

Table 4.17 Convenient Working Hours of the Digital Knowledge Centers

S.No	Description	Working days				Holidays			
		Mean	**Std.**	**Median**	**Verbal scale**	**Mean**	**Std.**	**Median**	**Verbal scale**
					Type of University				
1	Central	1.23	.673	1.00	Morning	2.43	.907	2.00	Noon
2	State	2.05	.629	2.00	Noon	2.47	.904	2.00	Noon
3	Deemed	1.87	.645	2.00	Noon	2.48	.895	2.00	Noon
					Category				
1	Research Scholars	1.86	.680	2.00	Noon	2.49	.905	2.00	Noon
2	Faculty Members	1.90	.675	2.00	Noon	2.43	.881	2.00	Noon
					Gender				
1	Male	1.92	.651	2.00	Noon	2.48	.901	2.00	Noon
2	Female	1.76	.724	2.00	Noon	2.46	.892	2.00	Noon
					Overall				
	Total	1.87	.679	2.00	Noon	2.47	.898	2.00	Noon

Table 4.17 and Figure 4.9 denotes that the overall preference of all categories of respondents indicate that the most optimum time for digital resource center is noon session on both working and holidays.

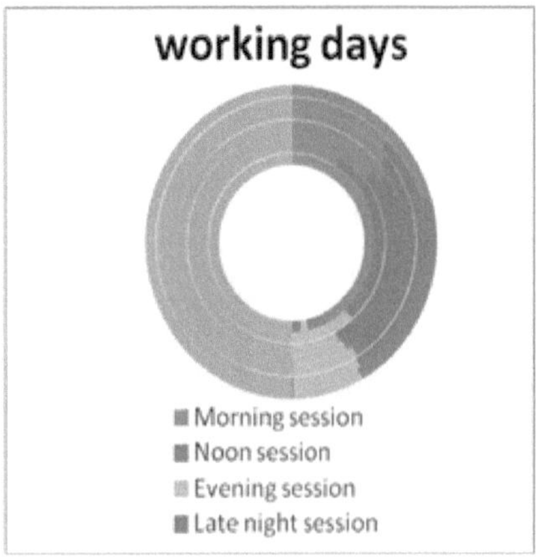

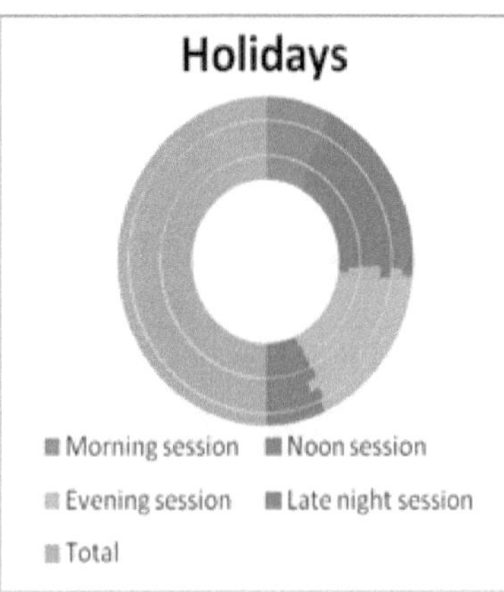

Figure 4.9 Convenient Working Hours on Working days and holidays

4.5 ESSENTIALITY OF DIGITAL KNOWLEDGE MANAGEMENT

Digital Knowledge Management is essential in this information explosion scenario and the changes need to be dynamic and revisited time to time to cater the need of the user more appropriately. Therefore the essentiality of Digital Knowledge Management is divided in to five major heads namely :

- Digital resources
- Digital services
- Digital user centric services
- Digital tools
- Digital service provides

4.5.1 Digital Resources

Users have indicated that the essentiality of the following digital resources on "agree" and "disagree" scales. Table 4.18 indicates the overall all responses on digital resources with number of responses, its percentage and ranked according to the percentage of response.

Table 4.18 Digital Resources

S.No	Database	Agree		Rank	Disagree		Rank
		Count	%		Count	%	
1	IEEE online	1369	66.6%	1	688	33.4%	10
2	ASME	1033	50.2%	8	1024	49.8%	2
3	ASCE	1295	63.0%	2	762	37.0%	8
4	Springer Link	1033	50.2%	8	1024	49.8%	2
5	JCCC	1061	51.6%	7	996	48.4%	4
6	EBSCO	1134	55.1%	6	923	44.9%	5
7	Emerald	1162	56.5%	5	895	43.5%	6
8	Science Direct	1207	58.7%	4	850	41.3%	7
9	Proquest	510	24.8%	10	1547	75.2%	1
10	ACM	1295	63.0%	2	762	37.0%	8

On an average more than 55% of respondents have responded that the following resources are essential and among them IEEE online (66.6%) was indicated at higher side followed by ASCE and ACM (63%). Proquest was indicated at least preference (24.8%).

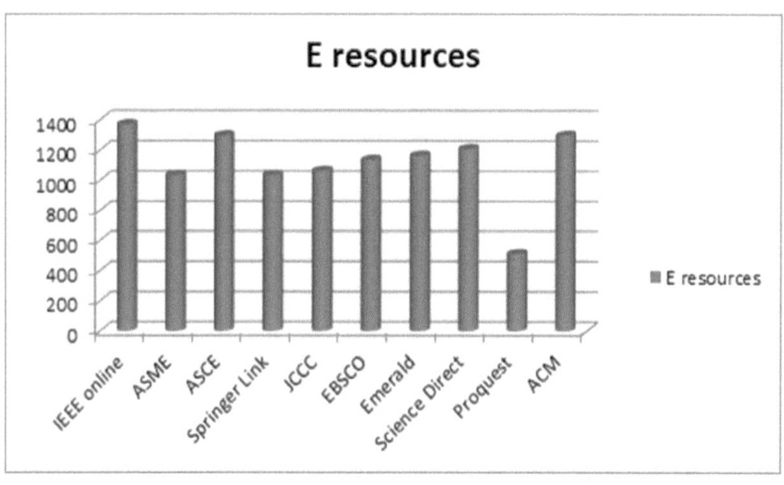

Figure 4.10 Digital Resources

Table 4.19 Digital Resources Vs Type of University

S.No	Database	Opinion	Central University		State University		Deemed University		Total	
1	IEEE online	Agree	182	8.8%	450	21.9%	737	35.8%	1369	66.6%
		Disagree	10	.5%	211	10.3%	467	22.7%	688	33.4%
2	ASME	Agree	121	5.9%	323	15.7%	589	28.6%	1033	50.2%
		Disagree	71	3.5%	338	16.4%	615	29.9%	1024	49.8%
3	ASCE	Agree	172	8.4%	419	20.4%	704	34.2%	1295	63.0%
		Disagree	20	1.0%	242	11.8%	500	24.3%	762	37.0%
4	Springer Link	Agree	121	5.9%	323	15.7%	589	28.6%	1033	50.2%
		Disagree	71	3.5%	338	16.4%	615	29.9%	1024	49.8%
5	JCCC	Agree	135	6.6%	333	16.2%	593	28.8%	1061	51.6%
		Disagree	57	2.8%	328	15.9%	611	29.7%	996	48.4%
6	EBSCO	Agree	135	6.6%	372	18.1%	627	30.5%	1134	55.1%
		Disagree	57	2.8%	289	14.0%	577	28.1%	923	44.9%
7	Emerald Disagree	Agree	138	6.7%	373	18.1%	651	31.6%	1162	56.5%
		Disagree	54	2.6%	288	14.0%	553	26.9%	895	43.5%
8	Science Direct	Agree	138	6.7%	394	19.2%	675	32.8%	1207	58.7%
		Disagree	54	2.6%	267	13.0%	529	25.7%	850	41.3%
9	Proquest	Agree	57	2.8%	367	17.8%	86	4.2%	510	24.8%
		Disagree	135	6.6%	294	14.3%	1118	54.4%	1547	75.2%
10	ACM	Agree	172	8.4%	419	20.4%	704	34.2%	1295	63.0%
		Disagree	20	1.0%	242	11.8%	500	24.3%	762	37.0%

From *Table 4.19,* we could infer that IEEE online was indicated as first essential database followed by ACM and ASCE database uniformly Science direct was indicated as third important requisite and the order of preference was uniform among all the type of universities. Least preference was indicated as Proquest by Central and Deemed Universities, ASME and springer link by state owned universities.

Table 4.20 Digital Resources Vs Category of User

S. No	Database	Opinion	Research Scholars		Faculty Members		Total	
1	IEEE online	Agree	958	46.6%	411	20.0%	1369	66.6%
		Disagree	484	23.5%	204	9.9%	688	33.4%
2	ASME	Agree	730	35.5%	303	14.7%	1033	50.2%
		Disagree	712	34.6%	312	15.2%	1024	49.8%
3	ASCE	Agree	903	43.9%	392	19.1%	1295	63.0%
		Disagree	539	26.2%	223	10.8%	762	37.0%
4	Springer Link	Agree	730	35.5%	303	14.7%	1033	50.2%
		Disagree	712	34.6%	312	15.2%	1024	49.8%
5	JCCC	Agree	750	36.5%	311	15.1%	1061	51.6%
		Disagree	692	33.6%	304	14.8%	996	48.4%
6	EBSCO	Agree	804	39.1%	330	16.0%	1134	55.1%
		Disagree	638	31.0%	285	13.9%	923	44.9%
7	Emerald	Agree	826	40.2%	336	16.3%	1162	56.5%
		Disagree	616	29.9%	279	13.6%	895	43.5%
8	Science Direct	Agree	854	41.5%	353	17.2%	1207	58.7%
		Disagree	588	28.6%	262	12.7%	850	41.3%
9	Proquest	Agree	316	15.4%	194	9.4%	510	24.8%
		Disagree	1126	54.7%	421	20.5%	1547	75.2%
10	ACM	Agree	903	43.9%	392	19.1%	1295	63.0%
		Disagree	539	26.2%	223	10.8%	762	37.0%

Table 4.20 indicates the responses on digital resources given by the two categories namely Research scholar and faculty members. All the respondents uniformly have indicated that IEEE online is more essential followed by ASCE and ACM. Thirdly Science direct and least preference was indicated as Proquest database.

Table 4.21 Digital Resources Vs Gender

S.No	Database	Opinion	Male		Female		Total	
1	IEEE	Agree	938	45.6%	431	21.0%	1369	66.6%
	online	Disagree	471	22.9%	217	10.5%	688	33.4%
2	ASME	Agree	716	34.8%	317	15.4%	1033	50.2%
		Disagree	693	33.7%	331	16.1%	1024	49.8%
3	ASCE	Agree	886	43.1%	409	19.9%	1295	63.0%
		Disagree	523	25.4%	239	11.6%	762	37.0%
4	Springer	Agree	716	34.8%	317	15.4%	1033	50.2%
	Link	Disagree	693	33.7%	331	16.1%	1024	49.8%
5	JCCC	Agree	735	35.7%	326	15.8%	1061	51.6%
		Disagree	674	32.8%	322	15.7%	996	48.4%
6	EBSCO	Agree	788	38.3%	346	16.8%	1134	55.1%
		Disagree	621	30.2%	302	14.7%	923	44.9%
7	Emerald	Agree	806	39.2%	356	17.3%	1162	56.5%
		Disagree	603	29.3%	292	14.2%	895	43.5%
8	Science	Agree	835	40.6%	372	18.1%	1207	58.7%
	Direct	Disagree	574	27.9%	276	13.4%	850	41.3%
9	Proquest	Agree	343	16.7%	167	8.1%	510	24.8%
		Disagree	1066	51.8%	481	23.4%	1547	75.2%
10	ACM	Agree	886	43.1%	409	19.9%	1295	63.0%
		Disagree	523	25.4%	239	11.6%	762	37.0%

Table 4.21 indicates that the respondents have indicated their preference uniformly. All the respondents from almost all the categories uniformly have indicated that IEEE online as first

preference followed by ASCE and ACM. Thirdly Science direct and least preference was indicated as Proquest database.

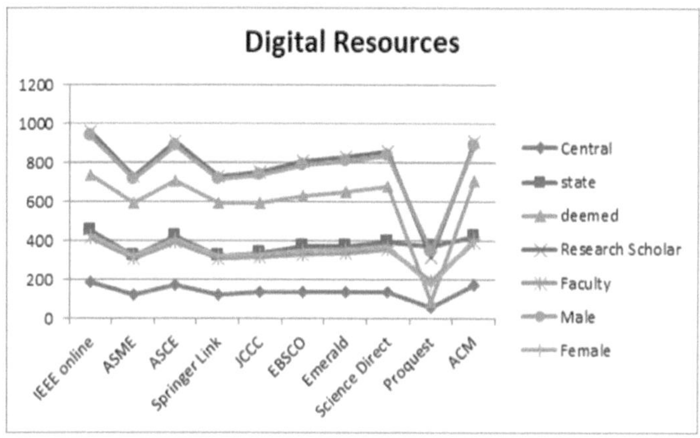

Figure 4.11 Digital Resources

Figure 4.11 shows the dependence of digital resources against different categories.

4.5.2 Digital Services

Different services rendered in university digital resource centres were analyzed on different categories of respondents like gender, type of university and category of the respondent on two scales namely "agree" and "disagree".

Table 4.22 Digital Knowledge Management Services

S.No	Description	Agree		Disagree	
1	E-literature search	1084	52.7%	973	47.3%
2	E-book services	1033	50.2%	1024	49.8%
3	E-abstracting/indexing	1249	60.7%	808	39.3%
4	E-newspaper	1477	71.8%	580	28.2%
5	Digital repository services	326	15.8%	1731	84.2%

S.No	Description	Agree		Disagree	
6	Digital content management services	1412	68.6%	645	31.4%
7	Downloading information from the internet	1781	86.6%	276	13.4%
	Total	8362		6037	

Table 4.22 shows the number of responses given with its percentage. Downloading of information from the internet was indicated as the first preference by many of the respondents. E-newspaper was indicated by 71.8% and digital content management services were indicated by 68.9% of respondents as essential. Essentiality of digital services was further analyzed with type of university, category of user and gender.

Table 4.23 Digital Services Vs Type of University

S. No	Digital Services	Opinion	Central University		State University		Deemed University		Total	
1	E-literature search	Agree	161	7.8%	187	9.1%	736	35.8%	1084	52.7%
		Disagree	31	1.5%	474	23.0%	468	22.8%	973	47.3%
2	E-book services	Agree	121	5.9%	323	15.7%	589	28.6%	1033	50.2%
		Disagree	71	3.5%	338	16.4%	615	29.9%	1024	49.8%
3	E-abstracting / indexing	Agree	182	8.8%	448	21.8%	619	30.1%	1249	60.7%
		Disagree	10	.5%	213	10.4%	585	28.4%	808	39.3%
4	E-newspaper	Agree	155	7.5%	609	29.6%	713	34.7%	1477	71.8%
		Disagree	37	1.8%	52	2.5%	491	23.9%	580	28.2%

S. No	Digital Services	Opinion	Central University		State University		Deemed University		Total	
5	Digital repository services	Agree	22	1.1%	20	1.0%	284	13.8%	326	15.8%
		Dis agree	170	8.3%	641	31.2%	920	44.7%	1731	84.2%
6	Digital content management services	Agree	105	5.1%	282	13.7%	1025	49.8%	1412	68.6%
		Dis agree	87	4.2%	379	18.4%	179	8.7%	645	31.4%
7	Down loading information from the internet	Agree	157	7.6%	611	29.7%	1013	49.2%	1781	86.6%
		Dis agree	35	1.7%	50	2.4%	191	9.3%	276	13.4%

***Table* 4.23** indicates that the respondents from Central Universities have indicated e-abstracting and indexing services followed by e-literature search and downloading of information from internet is the essential service expected from the digital resource center Respondents from state owned universities have indicated that downloading of information as essential requisite followed by e-newspaper, e-abstracting and indexing services. Deemed university respondents indicated that digital content management services as most essential followed by downloading of information and e-literature search. Order of essentiality differs with the type of university.

Table 4.24 Digital Services Vs Category of User

S. No	Description	Opinion	Research Scholars		Faculty Members		Total	
1	E-literature search	Agree	784	38.1%	300	14.6%	1084	52.7%
		Disagree	658	32.0%	315	15.3%	973	47.3%
2	E-book services	Agree	730	35.5%	303	14.7%	1033	50.2%
		Disagree	712	34.6%	312	15.2%	1024	49.8%
3	E-abstracting/ indexing	Agree	873	42.4%	376	18.3%	1249	60.7%
		Disagree	569	27.7%	239	11.6%	808	39.3%
4	E-newspaper	Agree	1016	49.4%	461	22.4%	1477	71.8%
		Disagree	426	20.7%	154	7.5%	580	28.2%
5	Digital repository services	Agree	247	12.0%	79	3.8%	326	15.8%
		Disagree	1195	58.1%	536	26.1%	1731	84.2%
6	Digital content management services	Agree	993	48.3%	419	20.4%	1412	68.6%
		Disagree	449	21.8%	196	9.5%	645	31.4%
7	Downloading information from the internet	Agree	1253	60.9%	528	25.7%	1781	86.6%
		Disagree	189	9.2%	87	4.2%	276	13.4%

Table 4.24 indicates that the research scholars have indicated downloading of information from the internet as essential service requisite followed by digital content management services. Faculty members have indicated downloading of information as first requisite followed by e-newspaper. Order of essentiality differs with the category of respondent.

Table 4.25 : Digital Services Vs Gender

S.No	Description	Opinion	Male		Female		Total	
1	E-literature search	Agree	747	36.3%	337	16.4%	1084	52.7%
		Disagree	662	32.2%	311	15.1%	973	47.3%
2	E-book services	Agree	716	34.8%	317	15.4%	1033	50.2%
		Disagree	693	33.7%	331	16.1%	1024	49.8%
3	E-abstr acting/ indexing	Agree	852	41.4%	397	19.3%	1249	60.7%
		Disagree	557	27.1%	251	12.2%	808	39.3%
4	E-news paper	Agree	967	47.0%	510	24.8%	1477	71.8%
		Disagree	442	21.5%	138	6.7%	580	28.2%
5	Digital repository services	Agree	223	10.8%	103	5.0%	326	15.8%
		Disagree	1186	57.7%	545	26.5%	1731	84.2%
6	Digital content manage ment services	Agree	978	47.5%	434	21.1%	1412	68.6%
		Disagree	431	21.0%	214	10.4%	645	31.4%
7	Down loading information from the internet	Agree	1222	59.4%	559	27.2%	1781	86.6%
		Disagree	187	9.1%	89	4.3%	276	13.4%

Table 4.25 indicates all the respondents without gender differentiation have indicated that downloading of information from the internet as essential service requisite followed by e-newspaper. Female respondents have indicated digital repository services as their second requisite. Least preference was indicated as digital repository by male and e-newspaper by female respondents.

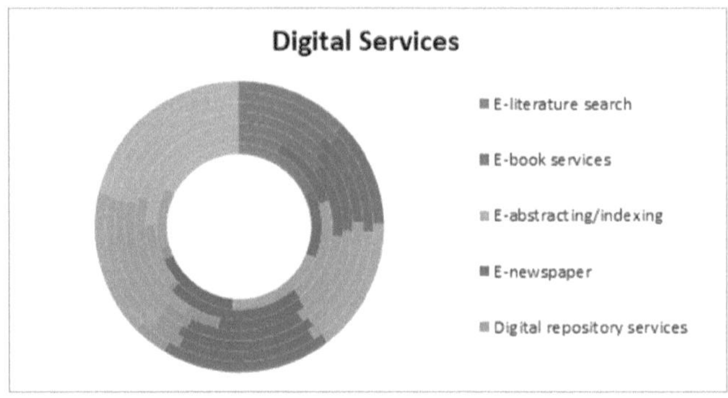

Figure 4.12 Digital Services

4.5.3 Digital User Centric Services

User centric services were estimated from respondents on "agree" and "disagree" scale on following 6 variables.

Table 4.26 Digital User Centric Services

S.No	Description	Agree		Disagree	
1	E-content management services	1324	64.4%	733	35.6%
2	E-question bank services	1066	51.8%	991	48.2%
3	library websites	1119	54.4%	938	45.6%
4	Knimbus, Ezproxy, Remote Access Services	1400	68.1%	657	31.9%
5	Library Automation	1336	64.9%	721	35.1%
6	Current Awareness Service	1460	71.0%	597	29.0%

Table 4.26 shows the overall responses given for the six variables among which Current Awareness Service was indicated as the more essential service followed by Ezproxy servers and library automation. Responses were further analyzed with respect to their gender, type of university and category.

Table 4.27 Digital User Centric Services Vs Type of University

S. No	Description	Opinion	Central University		State University		Deemed University		Total	
1	E-content management services	Agree	96	4.7%	538	26.2%	690	33.5%	1324	64.4%
		Dis agree	96	4.7%	123	6.0%	514	25.0%	733	35.6%
2	E-question bank services	Agree	106	5.2%	236	11.5%	724	35.2%	1066	51.8%
		Dis agree	86	4.2%	425	20.7%	480	23.3%	991	48.2%
3	Library web sites	Agree	159	7.7%	236	11.5%	724	35.2%	1119	54.4%
		Dis agree	33	1.6%	425	20.7%	480	23.3%	938	45.6%
4	Knim bus, Ezproxy, Remote Access Services	Agree	107	5.2%	538	26.2%	755	36.7%	1400	68.1%
		Dis agree	85	4.1%	123	6.0%	449	21.8%	657	31.9%
5	Library Automation	Agree	113	5.5%	542	26.3%	681	33.1%	1336	64.9%
		Dis agree	79	3.8%	119	5.8%	523	25.4%	721	35.1%
6	Current Awareness Services	Agree	158	7.7%	589	28.6%	713	34.7%	1460	71.0%
		Dis agree	34	1.7%	72	3.5%	491	23.9%	597	29.0%

Table 4.27 shows that the respondents from Central and State Universities have indicated library website as the first requisite followed by Current Awareness Services, whereas respondents from Deemed University have indicated Ezproxy servers as keen requisite followed by library website and e-question bank.

Table 4.28 Digital User Centric Services Vs Category of User

S.No	Description	Opinion	Research Scholars		Faculty Member		Total	
1	E-content management services	Agree	920	44.7%	404	19.6%	1324	64.4%
		Disagree	522	25.4%	211	10.3%	733	35.6%
2	E-question bank services	Agree	774	37.6%	292	14.2%	1066	51.8%
		Disagree	668	32.5%	323	15.7%	991	48.2%
3	library websites	Agree	813	39.5%	306	14.9%	1119	54.4%
		Disagree	629	30.6%	309	15.0%	938	45.6%
4	Knimbus, Ezproxy, Remote Access Services	Agree	972	47.3%	428	20.8%	1400	68.1%
		Disagree	470	22.8%	187	9.1%	657	31.9%
5	Library Automation	Agree	929	45.2%	407	19.8%	1336	64.9%
		Disagree	513	24.9%	208	10.1%	721	35.1%
6	Current Awareness Services	Agree	1003	48.8%	457	22.2%	1460	71.0%
		Disagree	439	21.3%	158	7.7%	597	29.0%

Table 4.28 shows that Current Awareness Services was indicated as most important requisite followed by Ezproxy by the two categories of respondents. Research scholars have indicated library websites and faculty members indicated library automation as third important requisite. Least preference was given toe-question bank services.

Table 4.29 Digital User Centric Services Vs Gender

S.No	Description	Opinion	Male		Female		Total	
1	E-content management services	Agree	882	42.9%	442	21.5%	1324	64.4%
		Disagree	527	25.6%	206	10.0%	733	35.6%
2	E-question bank services	Agree	744	36.2%	322	15.7%	1066	51.8%
		Disagree	665	32.3%	326	15.8%	991	48.2%
3	Library websites	Agree	775	37.7%	344	16.7%	1119	54.4%
		Disagree	634	30.8%	304	14.8%	938	45.6%
4	Knimbus, Ezproxy, Remote Access Services	Agree	919	44.7%	481	23.4%	1400	68.1%
		Disagree	490	23.8%	167	8.1%	657	31.9%
5	Library Automation	Agree	885	43.0%	451	21.9%	1336	64.9%
		Disagree	524	25.5%	197	9.6%	721	35.1%
6	Current Awareness Services	Agree	952	46.3%	508	24.7%	1460	71.0%
		Disagree	457	22.2%	140	6.8%	597	29.0%

Table 4.29 shows that Current Awareness Services was indicated as most important requisite followed by Ezproxy by all the respondents without gender bias. Male respondents and female respondents have indicated library automation as third important requisite. Least preference was given to e-question bank services.

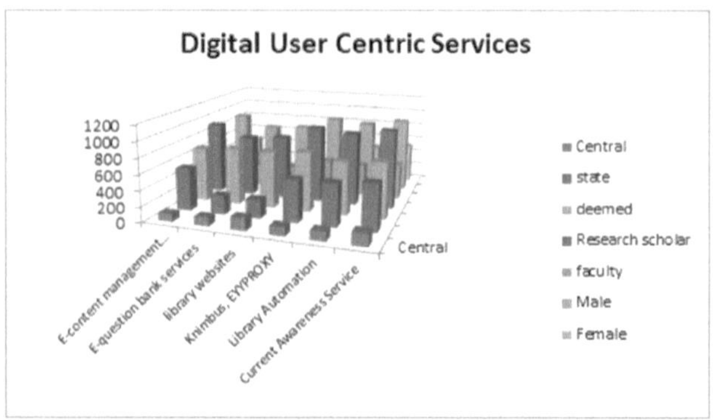

Figure 4.13 Digital User Centric Services

4.5.4 Digital Tools

Digital tools that are required to manage the digital resources and services. Respondents have indicated the requisites in two scales namely "agree" and "disagree".

Table 4.30 Digital Tool

S.No	Description	Agree		Disagree	
1	To send email to utilise library services	1384	67.3%	673	32.7%
2	University campus is Wi-Fi enabled	1037	50.4%	1020	49.6%
3	Online book reservation and renewal	1399	68.0%	658	32.0%
4	High speed internet access facilities	1473	71.6%	584	28.4%
5	Web OPAC	1366	66.4%	691	33.6%
6	Digital notice board	1478	71.9%	579	28.1%
7	Plasma TV	992	48.2%	1065	51.8%
8	Printing and scanning facility	1381	67.1%	676	32.9%

Table 4.30 indicates that digital notice board was indicated as preferred requisite followed by high speed internet access facilities and online book reservation and renewal.

Table 4.31 Digital Tools Vs Type of State

S.No	Description	Opinion	Central University		State University		Deemed University		Total	
1	To send email to utilise	Agree	136	6.6%	223	10.8%	1025	49.8%	1384	67.3%
	library services	Disagree	56	2.7%	438	21.3%	179	8.7%	673	32.7%
2	University campus is Wi-Fi	Agree	77	3.7%	236	11.5%	724	35.2%	1037	50.4%
	enabled ASME	Disagree	115	5.6%	425	20.7%	480	23.3%	1020	49.6%
3	Online book reservation and	Agree	104	5.1%	282	13.7%	1013	49.2%	1399	68.0%
	renewal	Disagree	88	4.3%	379	18.4%	191	9.3%	658	32.0%
4	High speed internet access	Agree	185	9.0%	598	29.1%	690	33.5%	1473	71.6%
	facilities	Disagree	7	.3%	63	3.1%	514	25.0%	584	28.4%
5	Web OPAC	Agree	93	4.5%	583	28.3%	690	33.5%	1366	66.4%
		Disagree	99	4.8%	78	3.8%	514	25.0%	691	33.6%
6	Digital notice board	Agree	153	7.4%	607	29.5%	718	34.9%	1478	71.9%
		Disagree	39	1.9%	54	2.6%	486	23.6%	579	28.1%
7	Plasma TV	Agree	79	3.8%	200	9.7%	713	34.7%	992	48.2%
		Disagree	113	5.5%	461	22.4%	491	23.9%	1065	51.8%
8	Printing and scanning	Agree	98	4.8%	281	13.7%	1002	48.7%	1381	67.1%
	facility	Disagree	94	4.6%	380	18.5%	202	9.8%	676	32.9%

Table 4.31 indicates that respondents from Central Universities have indicated internet access as prime requisite followed by digital notice board and email facilities to utilize library services. Preferences vary with the type of university. State owned university respondents have indicated that digital notice board as first preference followed by high speed internet access and email communication to utilize library services. Deemed university respondents have indicated email facility to utilize library services followed by library book reservation and renewal and printing and scanning facility.

Table 4.32 Digital Tools Vs Category of User

S.No	Description	Opinion	Research Scholars		Faculty Members		Total	
1	To send email to utilize library services	Agree	968	47.1%	416	20.2%	1384	67.3%
		Dis agree	474	23.0%	199	9.7%	673	32.7%
2	University campus is Wi-Fi enabled ASME	Agree	759	36.9%	278	13.5%	1037	50.4%
		Dis agree	683	33.2%	337	16.4%	1020	49.6%
3	Online book reservation and renewal	Agree	982	47.7%	417	20.3%	1399	68.0%
		Dis agree	460	22.4%	198	9.6%	658	32.0%
4	High speed internet access facilities	Agree	1017	49.4%	456	22.2%	1473	71.6%
		Dis agree	425	20.7%	159	7.7%	584	28.4%
5	Web OPAC	Agree	948	46.1%	418	20.3%	1366	66.4%
		Disagree	494	24.0%	197	9.6%	691	33.6%
6	Digital notice board	Agree	1017	49.4%	461	22.4%	1478	71.9%
		Disagree	425	20.7%	154	7.5%	579	28.1%
7	Plasma TV	Agree	716	34.8%	276	13.4%	992	48.2%
		Disagree	726	35.3%	339	16.5%	1065	51.8%
8	Printing and scanning facility	Agree	967	47.0%	414	20.1%	1381	67.1%
		Disagree	475	23.1%	201	9.8%	676	32.9%

Table 4.32 indicates that research scholars have given equal importance to digital notice board and high speed internet access followed by online book reservation and renewal system. Faculty members have indicated the same variables and preferences but faculty members have given importance to web OPAC.

Table 4.33 Digital Tools Vs Gender

S. No	Description	Opinion	Male		Female		Total	
1	To send email to utilize library services	Agree	954	46.4%	430	20.9%	1384	67.3%
		Disagree	455	22.1%	218	10.6%	673	32.7%
2	University campus is Wi-Fi enabled ASME	Agree	726	35.3%	311	15.1%	1037	50.4%
		Disagree	683	33.2%	337	16.4%	1020	49.6%
3	Online book reservation and renewal	Agree	965	46.9%	434	21.1%	1399	68.0%
		Disagree	444	21.6%	214	10.4%	658	32.0%
4	High speed internet access facilities	Agree	966	47.0%	507	24.6%	1473	71.6%
		Disagree	443	21.5%	141	6.9%	584	28.4%
5	Web OPAC	Agree	900	43.8%	466	22.7%	1366	66.4%
		Disagree	509	24.7%	182	8.8%	691	33.6%
6	Digital notice board	Agree	965	46.9%	513	24.9%	1478	71.9%
		Disagree	444	21.6%	135	6.6%	579	28.1%
7	Plasma TV	Agree	688	33.4%	304	14.8%	992	48.2%
		Disagree	721	35.1%	344	16.7%	1065	51.8%
8	Printing and scanning facility	Agree	948	46.1%	433	21.1%	1381	67.1%
		Disagree	461	22.4%	215	10.5%	676	32.9%

Table 4.33 shows the gender-wise responses to the variables of digital tool requisites. Male respondents have indicated high speed internet access facilities as top priority followed by online book reservation and renewal and digital notice board while female respondents have indicated digital notice board as first priority followed by high speed internet access facilities. Least preference was indicated as plasma by all the respondents invariably.

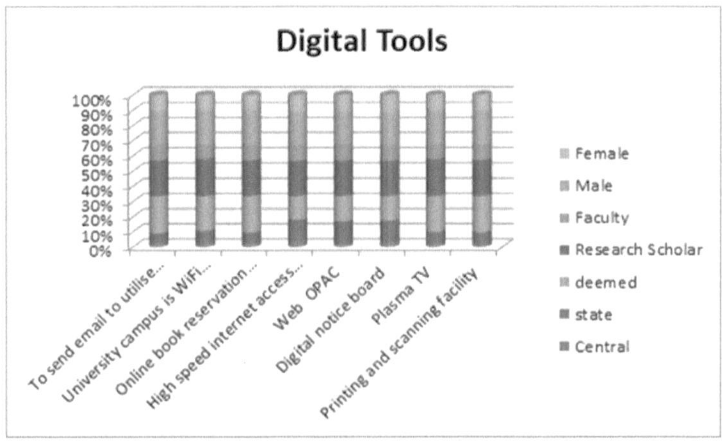

Figure 4.14 Digital Tools

4.5.5 Digital Service Providers

Table 4.34 shows the digital service providers. Respondents have indicated their responses in two scales namely "agree" and "disagree". No. of respondents and their percentages are listed in Table 4.33.

Table 4.34 Digital Services Providers

S.No	Digital Services	Agree		Disagree	
1	Study material through web portal	726	35.3%	1331	64.7%
2	National Knowledge Network (NKN)	997	48.5%	1060	51.5%
3	Spoken Tutorial IIT Bombay	1315	63.9%	742	36.1%
4	Networking facilities	1379	67.0%	678	33.0%
5	Open Access Knowledge Resources Material	1312	63.8%	745	36.2%
6	Federated Search Engine Facilities	1465	71.2%	592	28.8%
7	SMS alert service	1367	66.5%	690	33.5%
8	Social Network Services	1326	64.5%	731	35.5%
9	E-Mail Management	1349	65.6%	708	34.4%

From Table 4.34, it can be inferred that federated search engines facilities was indicated as top priority followed by networking facilities and SMS alert service. Least preference was given to study material through web portal.

Table 4.35 Digital Service Providers Vs Type of University

S.No	Description	Opinion	Central University		State University		Deemed University		Total	
1	Study material through web portal	Agree	102	5.0%	173	8.4%	451	21.9%	726	35.3%
		Disagree	90	4.4%	488	23.7%	753	36.6%	1331	64.7%
2	National Knowledge Network	Agree	72	3.5%	201	9.8%	724	35.2%	997	48.5%
	(NKN)	Disagree	120	5.8%	460	22.4%	480	23.3%	1060	51.5%
3	Spoken Tutorial IIT Bombay	Agree	101	4.9%	524	25.5%	690	33.5%	1315	63.9%
		Disagree	91	4.4%	137	6.7%	514	25.0%	742	36.1%
4	Networking facilities	Agree	116	5.6%	561	27.3%	702	34.1%	1379	67.0%
		Disagree	76	3.7%	100	4.9%	502	24.4%	678	33.0%
5	Open Access Knowledge Resources	Agree	93	4.5%	505	24.6%	714	34.7%	1312	63.8%
	Material	Disagree	99	4.8%	156	7.6%	490	23.8%	745	36.2%
6	Federated Search Engine Facilities	Agree	141	6.9%	573	27.9%	751	36.5%	1465	71.2%
		Disagree	51	2.5%	88	4.3%	453	22.0%	592	28.8%
7	SMS alert service	Agree	122	5.9%	251	12.2%	994	48.3%	1367	66.5%
		Disagree	70	3.4%	410	19.9%	210	10.2%	690	33.5%
8	Social Network Services	Agree	55	2.7%	270	13.1%	1001	48.7%	1326	64.5%
		Disagree	137	6.7%	391	19.0%	203	9.9%	731	35.5%
9	E-Mail Management	Agree	66	3.2%	282	13.7%	1001	48.7%	1349	65.6%
		Disagree	126	6.1%	379	18.4%	203	9.9%	708	34.4%

Federated search engine facilities, followed by SMS alert service and networking facilities was the order of preference by the respondents from Central University. State owned university respondents have indicated federated search engine facility, followed by networking facilities and spoken tutorial of IIT Bombay. Deemed university respondents have indicated social network services and email management as the top priority followed by SMS alert service. Study material through web portal was the least preference by respondents from State and Deemed University. The study was further extended to category of user.

Table 4.36 Digital Service Providers Vs Type of User

S. No	Description	Opinion	Research Scholars		Faculty Members		Total	
1	Study material through web portal	Agree	513	24.9%	213	10.4%	726	35.3%
		Disagree	929	45.2%	402	19.5%	1331	64.7%
2	National Knowledge Network (NKN)	Agree	726	35.3%	271	13.2%	997	48.5%
		Disagree	716	34.8%	344	16.7%	1060	51.5%
3	Spoken Tutorial IIT Bombay	Agree	908	44.1%	407	19.8%	1315	63.9%
		Disagree	534	26.0%	208	10.1%	742	36.1%
4	Networking facilities	Agree	952	46.3%	427	20.8%	1379	67.0%
		Disagree	490	23.8%	188	9.1%	678	33.0%
5	Open Access Knowledge Resources Material	Agree	907	44.1%	405	19.7%	1312	63.8%
		Disagree	535	26.0%	210	10.2%	745	36.2%

S. No	Description	Opinion	Research Scholars		Faculty Members		Total	
6	Federated Search Engine Facilities	Agree	1008	49.0%	457	22.2%	1465	71.2%
		Disagree	434	21.1%	158	7.7%	592	28.8%
7	SMS alert service	Agree	953	46.3%	414	20.1%	1367	66.5%
		Disagree	489	23.8%	201	9.8%	690	33.5%
8	Social Network Services	Agree	934	45.4%	392	19.1%	1326	64.5%
		Disagree	508	24.7%	223	10.8%	731	35.5%
9	E-Mail Management	Agree	954	46.4%	395	19.2%	1349	65.6%
		Disagree	488	23.7%	220	10.7%	708	34.4%

Table 4.35 indicates that Research scholar has focused on federated search engine facilities, followed by E-mail management and SMS alert service. Least importance was given to study material through web portal. Faculty members have indicated federated search engine facilities, followed by networking facilities and SMS alert services. There exists difference in the opinion among category of respondents. The study was further extended to gender of the respondent.

Table 4.37 : Digital Service Providers Vs Gender

S. No	Description	Opinion	Male		Female		Total	
1	Study material through web portal	Agree	483	23.5%	243	11.8%	726	35.3%
		Disagree	926	45.0%	405	19.7%	1331	64.7%
2	National Knowledge Network (NKN)	Agree	697	33.9%	300	14.6%	997	48.5%
		Disagree	712	34.6%	348	16.9%	1060	51.5%

S. No	Description	Opinion	Male		Female		Total	
3	Spoken Tutorial IIT Bombay	Agree	863	42.0%	452	22.0%	1315	63.9%
		Disagree	546	26.5%	196	9.5%	742	36.1%
4	Networking facilities	Agree	916	44.5%	463	22.5%	1379	67.0%
		Disagree	493	24.0%	185	9.0%	678	33.0%
5	Open Access Knowledge Resources Material	Agree	863	42.0%	449	21.8%	1312	63.8%
		Disagree	546	26.5%	199	9.7%	745	36.2%
6	Federated Search Engine Facilities	Agree	967	47.0%	498	24.2%	1465	71.2%
		Disagree	442	21.5%	150	7.3%	592	28.8%
7	SMS alert service	Agree	939	45.6%	428	20.8%	1367	66.5%
		Disagree	470	22.8%	220	10.7%	690	33.5%
8	Social Network Services	Agree	921	44.8%	405	19.7%	1326	64.5%
		Disagree	488	23.7%	243	11.8%	731	35.5%
9	E-Mail Management	Agree	938	45.6%	411	20.0%	1349	65.6%
		Disagree	471	22.9%	237	11.5%	708	34.4%

Table 4.36 indicates that male respondents have indicated that federated search engine facilities, followed by SMS alert service and Email management. Least importance was given to study material through web portal. Faculty members have indicated federated search engine facilities, followed by networking facilities and spoken tutorial by IIT Bombay. There exists difference in the opinion depending on gender.

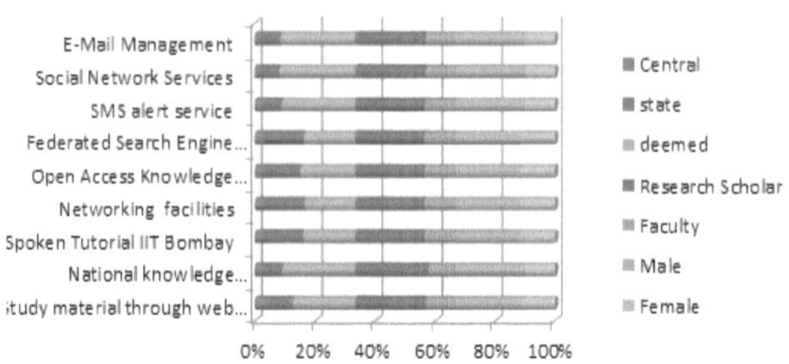

Figure 4.15 Digital Service Providers

4.5.6 Digital Service Policy

Digital service policy was analyzed using 10 variables with two scales namely "agree" and "disagree". ***Table 4.38*** indicates the responses with its percentage of responses.

Table 4.38 Digital Service Policy

S.No	Description	Agree		Disagree	
1	Citation analysis	1179	57.3%	878	42.7%
2	Anti-Plagiarism service	20	1.0%	2037	99.0%
3	Digital Copy rights issue service	7	.3%	2050	99.7%
4	Google scholar uploading service	16	.8%	2041	99.2%
5	Research Gate uploading service	21	1.0%	2036	99.0%
6	INFLIBNET Vidwan	0	.0%	2057	100.0%
7	Impact Factor, H-Index, Calculating service	18	.9%	2039	99.1%
8	Scholarly information	49	2.4%	2008	97.6%
9	Conference alert services	52	2.5%	2005	97.5%
10	Commercial Reference Management Tools and services	1180	57.4%	877	42.6%

From Table 4.38 it can be inferred that commercial reference management tools & services was indicated as the most important requisite followed by citation analysis and importance was not given to INFLIBNET Vidwan. The study was further analyzed with type of university, gender and category of the respondent.

Table 4.39 Digital Service Policy Vs Type of University

S.No	Description	Opinion	Central University		State University		Deemed University		Total	
1	Citation analysis	Agree	169	8.2%	424	20.6%	586	28.5%	1179	57.3%
		Disagree	23	1.1%	237	11.5%	618	30.0%	878	42.7%
2	Anti-Plagiarism service	Agree	20	1.0%	0	0.0%	0	0.0%	20	1.0%
		Disagree	172	8.4%	661	32.1%	1204	58.5%	2037	99.0%
3	Digital Copy rights Issue service	Agree	3	.1%	0	0.0%	4	.2%	7	.3%
		Disagree	189	9.2%	661	32.1%	1200	58.3%	2050	99.7%
4	Google scholar uploading service	Agree	1	.0%	15	.7%	0	0.0%	16	.8%
		Disagree	191	9.3%	646	31.4%	1204	58.5%	2041	99.2%
5	Research Gate uploading service	Agree	18	.9%	0	0.0%	3	.1%	21	1.0%
		Disagree	174	8.5%	661	32.1%	1201	58.4%	2036	99.0%
6	INFLIB NET Vidwan	Agree	0	0.0%	0	0.0%	0	0.0%	0	0.0%
		Disagree	192	9.3%	661	32.1%	1204	58.5%	2057	100.0%
7	Impact Factor, H-Index, Calculating service	Agree	3	.1%	0	0.0%	15	.7%	18	.9%
		Disagree	189	9.2%	661	32.1%	1189	57.8%	2039	99.1%
8	Scholarly information	Agree	38	1.8%	1	.0%	10	.5%	49	2.4%
		Disagree	154	7.5%	660	32.1%	1194	58.0%	2008	97.6%
9	Conference alert services	Agree	13	.6%	28	1.4%	11	.5%	52	2.5%
		Disagree	179	8.7%	633	30.8%	1193	58.0%	2005	97.5%
10	Commercial Reference Management Tools and services	Agree	152	7.4%	377	18.3%	651	31.6%	1180	57.4%
		Disagree	40	1.9%	284	13.8%	553	26.9%	877	42.6%

Table 4.39 indicates that the citation analysis was given first preference by Central and State Universities. Deemed universities have indicated commercial reference management tool and services as their top requisite which was indicated as second preference by the Central and State Universities. Scholarly information, conference alert services and impact factor H index calculating services was third preference indicated by Central, State and Deemed University respondents respectively.

Table 4.40 Digital Service Policy Vs Category of User

S.No	Description	Opinion	Research Scholars		Faculty Members		Total	
1	Citation analysis	Agree	797	38.7%	382	18.6%	1179	57.3%
		Disagree	645	31.4%	233	11.3%	878	42.7%
2	Anti-Plagiarism service	Agree	10	.5%	10	.5%	20	1.0%
		Disagree	1432	69.6%	605	29.4%	2037	99.0%
3	Digital Copy rights Issue service	Agree	6	.3%	1	.0%	7	.3%
		Disagree	1436	69.8%	614	29.8%	2050	99.7%
4	Google scholar uploading service	Agree	11	.5%	5	.2%	16	.8%
		Disagree	1431	69.6%	610	29.7%	2041	99.2%
5	Research Gate uploading service	Agree	17	.8%	4	.2%	21	1.0%
		Disagree	1425	69.3%	611	29.7%	2036	99.0%
6	INFLIBNET Vidwan	Agree	0	0.0%	0	0.0%	0	0.0%
		Disagree	1442	70.1%	615	29.9%	2057	100.0%

S.No	Description	Opinion	Research Scholars		Faculty Members		Total	
7	Impact Factor, H-Index, Calculating service	Agree	11	.5%	7	.3%	18	.9%
		Disagree	1431	69.6%	608	29.6%	2039	99.1%
8	Scholarly information	Agree	40	1.9%	9	.4%	49	2.4%
		Disagree	1402	68.2%	606	29.5%	2008	97.6%
9	Conference alert services	Agree	39	1.9%	13	.6%	52	2.5%
		Disagree	1403	68.2%	602	29.3%	2005	97.5%
10	Commercial Reference Management Tools and services	Agree	840	40.8%	340	16.5%	1180	57.4%
		Disagree	602	29.3%	275	13.4%	877	42.6%

Table 4.40 indicates that there exists difference between the order of preferences on digital service policy among the respondents with reference to the category of the respondent. Commercial reference management tool and services, followed by citation analysis and scholarly information was indicated as the order of preference by research scholars where as citation analysis was given importance by faculty members followed by commercial reference management tools and services and conference alert services. Least preference was indicated as anti-plagiarism by the research scholars and INFLIBNET Vidwan by the faculty members.

Table 4.41 Digital Service Policy Vs Gender

S.No	Description	Opinion	Male		Female		Total	
1	Citation analysis	Agree	801	38.9%	378	18.4%	1179	57.3%
		Disagree	608	29.6%	270	13.1%	878	42.7%
2	Anti-Plagiarism service	Agree	6	.3%	14	.7%	20	1.0%
		Disagree	1403	68.2%	634	30.8%	2037	99.0%
3	Digital Copy rights Issue service	Agree	6	.3%	1	.0%	7	.3%
		Disagree	1403	68.2%	647	31.5%	2050	99.7%
4	Google scholar uploading service	Agree	12	.6%	4	.2%	16	.8%
		Disagree	1397	67.9%	644	31.3%	2041	99.2%
5	Research Gate uploading service	Agree	12	.6%	9	.4%	21	1.0%
		Disagree	1397	67.9%	639	31.1%	2036	99.0%
6	INFLIBNET Vidwan	Agree	0	0.0%	0	0.0%	0	0.0%
		Disagree	1409	68.5%	648	31.5%	2057	100.0%
7	Impact Factor, H-Index, Calculating service	Agree	12	.6%	6	.3%	18	.9%
		Disagree	1397	67.9%	642	31.2%	2039	99.1%
8	Scholarly information	Agree	32	1.6%	17	.8%	49	2.4%
		Disagree	1377	66.9%	631	30.7%	2008	97.6%
9	Conference alert services	Agree	41	2.0%	11	.5%	52	2.5%
		Disagree	1368	66.5%	637	31.0%	2005	97.5%
10	Commer cial Refer ence Manage ment Tools and services	Agree	817	39.7%	363	17.6%	1180	57.4%
		Disagree	592	28.8%	285	13.9%	877	42.6%

Table 4.41 indicates that there exists difference between the orders of preference on digital service policy among gender of respondents. Commercial reference management tool and services, followed by citation analysis and conference alert services was indicated as the order of preference by male respondents whereas citation analysis was given importance by female respondents followed by commercial reference management tools and services and scholarly information. Least preference was indicated as INFLIBNET Vidwan by all the respondents uniformly.

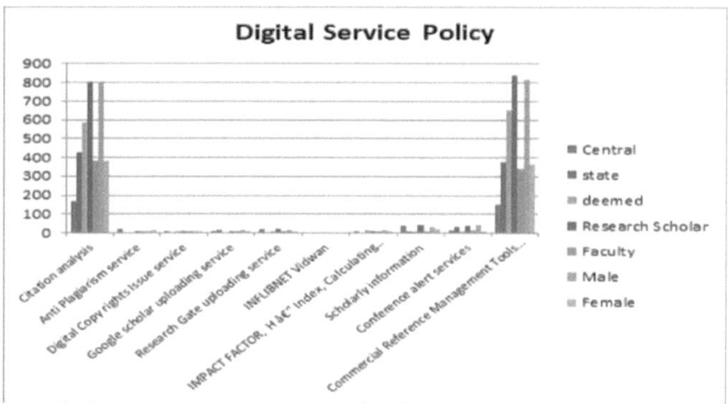

Figure 4.16 : Digital Service Policy

4.6 DEPENDENCE

Technological dependence is vital on Digital knowledge management and the changes required to be designed to the changes time to time to cater the need. Dependence of Digital Knowledge Management is divided in to six major heads namely:

- Digital Resources
- Digital Services
- Digital User Centric Services
- Digital Tools
- Digital Service Provides
- Digital Service Policy

4.6.1 Digital Resources

Dependence on digital resources was estimated on four scales namely "No dependence", "rare dependence", "occasional" and "frequently". Responses were tabulated, mean and standard deviation was calculated. Higher mean and lower deviation was given higher rank.

Table 4.42 Digital Resources Dependence

S.No	Database	No Dependence		Rare Dependence		Occasional		Frequently		Mean	Std.	Rank
1	IEEE online	0	.0%	0	.0%	16	.8%	2041	99.2%	3.99	.088	1
2	ASME	0	.0%	4	.2%	139	6.8%	1914	93.0%	3.93	.265	2
3	ASCE	29	1.4%	35	1.7%	198	9.6%	1795	87.3%	3.83	.511	4
4	Springer Link	3	.1%	56	2.7%	107	5.2%	1891	91.9%	3.89	.402	3
5	JCCC	12	.6%	55	2.7%	236	11.5%	1754	85.3%	3.81	.490	5
6	EBSCO	20	1.0%	315	15.3%	1057	51.4%	665	32.3%	3.15	.702	7
7	Emerald	37	1.8%	270	13.1%	1750	85.1%	0	.0%	2.83	.419	10
8	Science Direct	49	2.4%	343	16.7%	1533	74.5%	132	6.4%	2.85	.551	9
9	Proquest	25	1.2%	245	11.9%	1366	66.4%	421	20.5%	3.06	.607	8
10	ACM	12	.6%	16	.8%	805	39.1%	1224	59.5%	3.58	.543	6

IEEE online was depended more followed by SME and Springer Link. Emerald publishing was least depended. Mean ranges between 3.99 and 2.83, which indicate that the respondents have indicated occasional to frequent usage. Standard deviation ranges between 0.088 and 0.702 which indicates that there is no significant difference between the opinions between the respondents.

Table 4.43 Digital Resources Dependence Vs Type of University

S.No	Database	Central University			State University			Deemed University			Total		
		Mean	Std.	Rank	Mean	Std.	Rank	Mean	Std.	Rank	Mean	Std.	Rank
1	IEEE online	3.98	.124	2	3.99	.087	1	3.99	.081	1	3.99	.088	1
2	ASME	3.99	.102	1	3.79	.406	5	3.99	.115	2	3.93	.265	2
3	ASCE	3.71	.520	4	3.92	.396	3	3.80	.557	5	3.83	.511	4
4	Springer Link	3.98	.124	2	3.92	.265	2	3.85	.482	4	3.89	.402	3
5	JCCC	2.96	.945	6	3.89	.325	4	3.91	.287	3	3.81	.490	5
6	EBSCO	2.86	.761	7	3.16	.446	7	3.19	.792	7	3.15	.702	7
7	Emerald	2.59	.703	8	2.92	.275	9	2.82	.408	10	2.83	.419	10
8	Science Direct	2.45	.804	9	2.92	.278	10	2.87	.587	9	2.85	.551	9
9	Proquest	2.41	.710	10	3.05	.361	8	3.17	.631	8	3.06	.607	8
10	ACM	3.46	.670	5	3.44	.496	6	3.67	.525	6	3.58	.543	6

State and Deemed University respondents depended more on IEEE online followed by ASME and Springer Link. Central University respondents have indicated ASME followed by IEEE online and Springer Link. Proquest by Central Universities, Science direct by State Universities and Emerald by Deemed Universities were least depended on. The study was further extended to the category of user.

Table 4.44 Digital Resources Dependence Vs Category of User

S. No	Data base	Research Scholars			Faculty Members			Total		
		Mean	Std.	Rank	Mean	Std.	Rank	Mean	Std.	Rank
1	IEEE online	3.99	.087	1	3.99	.090	1	3.99	.088	1
2	ASME	3.95	.233	2	3.88	.325	3	3.93	.265	2
3	ASCE	3.82	.520	4	3.85	.491	4	3.83	.511	4
4	Spring er Link	3.88	.429	3	3.92	.330	2	3.89	.402	3
5	JCCC	3.81	.498	5	3.83	.470	5	3.81	.490	5
6	EBSCO	3.15	.718	7	3.15	.664	7	3.15	.702	7
7	Emer ald	2.83	.426	10	2.84	.400	10	2.83	.419	10
8	Science Direct	2.85	.570	9	2.85	.503	9	2.85	.551	9
9	Pro quest	3.08	.605	8	3.02	.610	8	3.06	.607	8
10	ACM	3.60	.540	6	3.52	.547	6	3.58	.543	6

From Table 4.44 it can be inferred that IEEE online was preferred uniformly by all categories. Research scholars indicated ASME as next preference followed by Springer Link. Faculty members indicated Springer Link followed by ASME. Least preference was indicated as Emerald by all the respondents uniformly.

Table 4.45 Digital Resources Dependence Vs Gender

S.No	Database	Male			Female			Total		
		Mean	**Std.**	**Rank**	**Mean**	**Std.**	**Rank**	**Mean**	**Std.**	**Rank**
1	IEEE online	3.99	.088	1	3.99	.088	1	3.99	.088	1
2	ASME	3.92	.280	2	3.95	.227	2	3.93	.265	2
3	ASCE	3.83	.517	5	3.81	.499	4	3.83	.511	4
4	Springer Link	3.89	.395	3	3.88	.419	3	3.89	.402	3
5	JCCC	3.83	.462	4	3.77	.542	5	3.81	.490	5
6	EBSCO	3.17	.723	7	3.11	.653	7	3.15	.702	7
7	Emerald	2.83	.417	10	2.83	.422	10	2.83	.419	10
8	Science Direct	2.85	.569	9	2.84	.511	9	2.85	.551	9
9	Proquest	3.09	.607	8	2.99	.604	8	3.06	.607	8
10	ACM	3.59	.528	6	3.54	.573	6	3.58	.543	6

From Table 4.45 depicts that IEEE online was preferred followed by ASME and Springer Link uniformly by all respondents and least preference was indicated as Emerald without gender bias. Overall ranks were tabulated for easy understanding and comparison in Table 4.46.

Table 4.46 Digital Resources Dependence – Overall Rank

S.No	Database	Overall	Central University	State University	Deemed University	Research Scholars	Faculty Members	Male	Female
1	IEEE Online	1	2	1	1	1	1	1	1
2	ASME	2	1	5	2	2	3	2	2
3	ASCE	4	4	3	5	4	4	5	4
4	Springer Link	3	2	2	4	3	2	3	3
5	JCCC	5	6	4	3	5	5	4	5
6	EBSCO	7	7	7	7	7	7	7	7
7	Emerald	10	8	9	10	10	10	10	10
8	Science Direct	9	9	10	9	9	9	9	9
9	Proquest	8	10	8	8	8	8	8	8
10	ACM	6	5	6	6	6	6	6	6

Figure 4.17 Digital Resources Dependence – Overall Rank

From Table 4.46 and Figure 4.16, it can be seen that the preference were uniform. IEEE online and ASME was indicated as first preference followed by Springer Link by most of the categories. Emerald as least preference.

4.6.2 Digital Services

Table 4.47 depicts digital services dependence in four scales namely "no dependence", "rare dependence", "occasional" and "frequently". Mean and standard deviation was calculated and the appropriate ranks were assigned for the seven variables to analyze the digital services dependence.

Table 4.47 Digital Services Dependence

S.No	Description	No Dependence		Rare Dependence		Occasional		Frequently		Mean	Std.	Rank
1	E-Literature Search	57	2.8%	616	29.9%	1318	64.1%	66	3.2%	2.68	.582	5
2	E-Book Services	31	1.5%	689	33.5%	1327	64.5%	10	.5%	2.64	.520	6
3	E-Abstracting/ Indexing	424	20.6%	689	33.5%	617	30.0%	327	15.9%	2.41	.986	7
4	E-Newspaper	54	2.6%	380	18.5%	1381	67.1%	242	11.8%	2.88	.627	3
5	Digital repository services	180	8.8%	346	16.8%	780	37.9%	751	36.5%	3.02	.940	1
6	Digital content management services	54	2.6%	380	18.5%	1381	67.1%	242	11.8%	2.88	.627	3
7	Downloading information from the internet	180	8.8%	346	16.8%	780	37.9%	751	36.5%	3.02	.940	1

From Table 4.47, it can be inferred that downloading of information from the internet was indicated as the first dependable service. Equal importance was given to digital repository services. Next preference was indicated as digital content management services and E-newspaper. Mean ranges between 3.99 and 2.83, which indicate that the respondents have indicated occasional to frequent usage. Standard deviation ranges between 0.088 and 0.702 which indicates that there is no significant difference between the opinions between the respondents. The study was further extended to the type of university.

Table 4.48 Digital Services Dependence Vs Type of University

S.	Description	Central University			State University			Deemed University			Total		
No		Mean	Std.	Rank	Mean	Std.	Rank	Mean	Std.	Rank	Mean	Std.	Rank
1	E-Literature search	2.74	.774	6	2.37	.675	6	2.83	.397	5	2.68	.582	5
2	E-Book services	2.17	.668	7	2.42	.498	7	2.83	.397	5	2.64	.520	6
3	E-Abstracting/ Indexing	3.25	1.018	1	1.97	1.052	5	2.52	.811	7	2.41	.986	7
4	E-Newspaper	2.95	1.263	4	2.87	.365	3	2.87	.587	3	2.88	.627	3
5	Digital repository services	2.95	.967	2	3.03	.940	1	3.03	.936	1	3.02	.940	1
6	Digital content management services	2.95	1.263	4	2.87	.365	3	2.87	.587	3	2.88	.627	3
7	Downloading information from the internet	2.95	.967	2	3.03	.940	1	3.03	.936	1	3.02	.940	1

Table 4.48 indicates that the central university respondents indicated that E-abstracting and indexing as their first preference followed by digital repository services and downloading of information from the internet as dependable services. State university and deemed university respondents have uniformly indicated digital repository services and downloading of information from the internet as their top preference followed by E-newspaper and digital content management services.

Table 4.49 Digital Services Dependence Vs Category of User

S.No	Description	Research Scholars			Faculty Members			Total		
		Mean	Std.	Rank	Mean	Std.	Rank	Mean	Std.	Rank
1	E-Literature search	2.67	.589	5	2.69	.566	5	2.68	.582	5
2	E-Book services	2.64	.521	6	2.64	.517	6	2.64	.520	6
3	E-Abstracting/ Indexing	2.39	1.006	7	2.46	.937	7	2.41	.986	7
4	E-Newspaper	2.87	.640	3	2.90	.597	3	2.88	.627	3
5	Digital repository services	3.03	.930	1	3.00	.963	1	3.02	.940	1
6	Digital content management services	2.87	.640	3	2.90	.597	3	2.88	.627	3
7	Downloading information from the internet	3.03	.930	1	3.00	.963	1	3.02	.940	1

The study was further extended to the category of user and gender. Research scholars and Faculty Members have uniformly indicated that downloading of information from the internet and digital repository services as top priority followed by digital content management services and e-newspapers. E-abstracting and indexing services were indicated as least preference. All the preferences were uniform.

Table 4.50 Digital Services Dependence Vs Gender

S. No	Description	Male			Female			Total		
		Mean	Std.	Rank	Mean	Std.	Rank	Mean	Std.	Rank
1	E-Literature search	2.67	.585	5	2.69	.574	5	2.68	.582	5
2	E-Book services	2.65	.518	6	2.61	.524	6	2.64	.520	6
3	E-Abstracting/indexing	2.37	.968	7	2.51	1.019	7	2.41	.986	7
4	E-Newspaper	2.87	.624	3	2.90	.633	3	2.88	.627	3
5	Digital repository services	3.02	.934	1	3.03	.952	1	3.02	.940	1
6	Digital content management services	2.87	.624	3	2.90	.633	3	2.88	.627	3
7	Downloading information from the internet	3.02	.934	1	3.03	.952	1	3.02	.940	1

Table 4.50 depicts that all the ranks and preferences were uniform and similar to category of respondent. Mean ranges between 3.02 and 2.37 for male and 3.03 and 2.51 for female, which indicates that the respondents have indicated occasional to frequent usage. Standard deviation ranges between 0.518 and 0.968 for male and 0.524 and 1.019 which indicates that there is no significant difference between the opinions between the respondents. The study was further extended to the type of university.

Table 4.51 Digital Services Dependence – Overall rank

S.No	Description	Overall	Central University	State University	Deemed University	Research Scholars	Faculty Members	Male	Female
1	E-Literature search	5	6	6	5	5	5	5	5
2	E-Book services	6	7	7	5	6	6	6	6
3	E-Abstracting/ Indexing	7	1	5	7	7	7	7	7
4	E-Newspaper	3	4	3	3	3	3	3	3
5	Digital repository services	1	2	1	1	1	1	1	1
6	Digital content management services	3	4	3	3	3	3	3	3
7	Downloading information from the internet	1	2	1	1	1	1	1	1

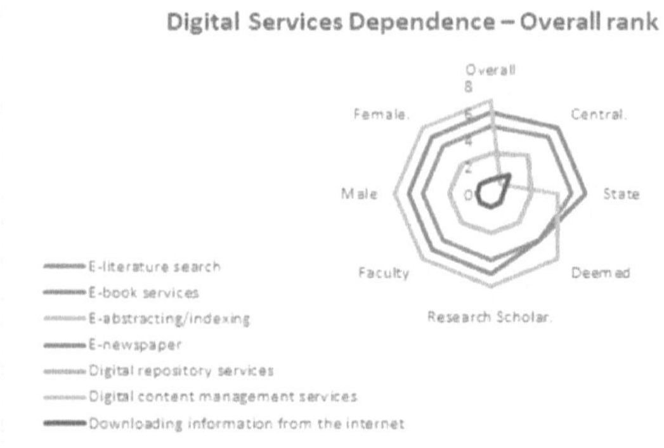

Figure 4.18 Digital Resources Dependence – Overall Rank

From Table 4.51 and Figure 4.17, it can be seen that the preference were uniform. Downloading of information from the internet and digital repository services was indicated as first preference by all the categories except the overall and respondents from Central University. E-abstracting and indexing services were indicated as least preference.

4.6.3 Digital User Centric Services

In Table 4.52, digital user centric services were analyzed in in five scales namely "no dependence", "rare dependence", "occasional", "frequently" and "high dependence". Mean and standard deviation was calculated and the appropriate ranks were assigned for the six variables to analyze the digital user centric services and user dependence.

Table 4.52 Digital User Centric Services Dependence

S. No	Description	No Dependence		Rare Dependence		Occasional		Frequently		High		Mean	Std.	Rank
1	E-content management services	12	.6%	17	.8%	92	4.5%	1936	94.1%	0	.0%	3.92	.352	1
2	E-question bank services	28	1.4%	78	3.8%	265	12.9%	1640	79.7%	46	2.2%	3.78	.613	2
3	library websites	67	3.3%	70	3.4%	317	15.4%	1603	77.9%	0	.0%	3.68	.694	3
4	Knimbus, Ezproxy, Remote Access Services	54	2.6%	380	18.5%	1381	67.1%	242	11.8%	0	.0%	2.88	.627	5
5	Library Automation	45	2.2%	425	20.7%	1213	59.0%	374	18.2%	0	.0%	2.93	.687	4
6	Current Awareness Services	31	1.5%	677	32.9%	1349	65.6%	0	.0%	0	.0%	2.64	.510	6

***Table* 4.52** indicates that E-content management services was indicated as first preference followed by Mean ranges between 3.99 and 2.83, which indicates that the respondents have indicated occasional to frequent usage. Standard deviation ranges between 0.088 and 0.702 which indicates that there is no significant difference between the opinions between the respondents. The study was further extended to the type of university.

Table 4.53 Digital User Centric Services Dependence Vs Type of University

S. No	Description	Central University			State University			Deemed University			Total		
		Mean	Std.	Rank	Mean	Std.	Rank	Mean	Std.	Rank	Mean	Std.	Rank
1	E-content management services	3.22	.854	1	3.99	.087	1	3.99	.081	1	3.92	.352	1
2	E-question bank services	2.32	.731	5	3.96	.431	2	3.91	.287	2	3.78	.613	2
3	library websites	2.87	.367	3	3.70	.824	3	3.80	.557	3	3.68	.694	3
4	Knimbus, Ezproxy, Remote Access Services	2.95	1.263	2	2.87	.365	4	2.87	.587	5	2.88	.627	5
5	Library Automation	2.41	.710	4	2.80	.456	5	3.09	.730	4	2.93	.687	4
6	Current Awareness Services	2.18	.591	6	2.42	.498	6	2.83	.397	6	2.64	.510	6

***Table* 4.53** indicates that E-content management services were indicated as first preference by respondents of all type of universities. Second preference was indicated as Ezproxy servers by Central University, e-question bank services by State and Deemed Universities. Third preference was indicated as library websites by respondents from all type of universities. Mean ranges between 3.22 and 2.18 for central, 3.99 and 2.42 for state and 3.99 and 2.83 for Deemed Universities, which indicates that the respondents have indicated occasional to frequent usage. Standard deviation ranges between 0.087 and 1.263 which indicates that there is no significant difference between the opinion between the respondents. The study was further extended to the category of user.

Table 4.54 Digital User Centric Services Dependence Vs Category of user

S.No	Description	Research Scholars			Faculty Members			Total		
		Mean	**Std.**	**Rank**	**Mean**	**Std.**	**Rank**	**Mean**	**Std.**	**Rank**
1	E-Content Management Services	3.93	.328	1	3.90	.402	1	3.92	.352	1
2	E-Question bank services	3.77	.609	2	3.80	.623	2	3.78	.613	2
3	Library websites	3.67	.705	3	3.70	.666	3	3.68	.694	3
4	Knimbus, Ezproxy, Remote Access Services	2.87	.640	5	2.90	.597	4	2.88	.627	5
5	Library Automation	2.97	.682	4	2.85	.690	5	2.93	.687	4
6	Current Awareness Services	2.64	.512	6	2.64	.507	6	2.64	.510	6

Table 4.54 indicates that E-content management services were indicated as first preference followed by e-question bank services & library websites by all categories of respondents uniformly. Mean ranges between 3.93 and 2.64 for research scholars and 3.90 and 2.64 for faculty members which indicate that the respondents have indicated occasional to frequent usage. Standard deviation ranges between 0.328 and 0.690 which indicates that there is no significant difference between the opinions between the respondents. The study was further extended to the gender of user.

Table 4.55 Digital User Centric Services Dependence Vs Gender

S. No	Description	Male			Female			Total		
		Mean	Std.	Rank	Mean	Std.	Rank	Mean	Std.	Rank
1	E-content management services	3.93	.361	1	3.91	.333	1	3.92	.352	1
2	E-question bank services	3.81	.566	2	3.71	.699	2	3.78	.613	2
3	Library websites	3.71	.680	3	3.61	.719	3	3.68	.694	3
4	Knimbus, Ezproxy, Remote Access Services	2.87	.624	5	2.90	.633	4	2.88	.627	5
5	Library Automation	2.97	.691	4	2.85	.672	5	2.93	.687	4
6	Current Awareness Services	2.65	.509	6	2.62	.514	6	2.64	.510	6

Table 4.55 indicates that an E-content management services were indicated as first preference followed by e-question bank services and library websites by all respondents uniformly without gender bias. Mean ranges between 3.93 and 2.65 for male respondents and 3.91 and 2.62 for female respondents which indicate that the respondents have indicated occasional to frequent usage. Standard deviation ranges between 0.352 and 0.694 which indicates that there is no significant difference between the opinions between the respondents.

Table 4.56 Digital User Centric Services Dependence - Overall

S.No	Description	Overall	Central University	State University	Deemed University	Research Scholars	Faculty Members	Male	Female
1	E-content management services	1	1	1	1	1	1	1	1
2	E-question bank services	2	5	2	2	2	2	2	2
3	library websites	3	3	3	3	3	3	3	3
4	Knimbus, Ezproxy, Remote Access Services	5	2	4	5	5	4	5	4
5	Library Automation	4	4	5	4	4	5	4	5
6	Current Awareness Services	6	6	6	6	6	6	6	6

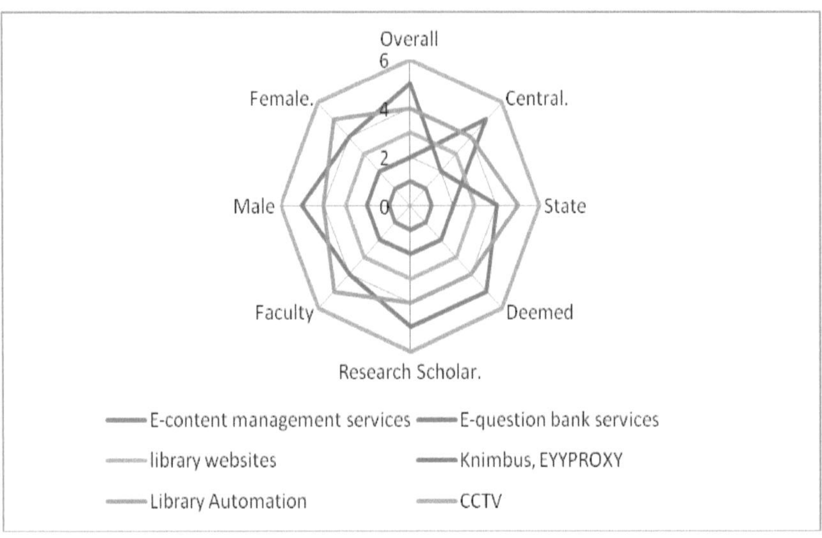

Figure 4.19 Digital Knowledge Management - Concepts

From ***Table 4.53 and Figure 4.19,*** it can be seen that the preferences were not uniform except the first preference as Current Awareness Service.

4.6.4 Digital Tools

In Table 4.57 dependence on digital tools were in four scales namely "no dependence", "rare dependence", "occasional" and "frequently". Mean and standard deviation was calculated and the appropriate ranks were assigned for the eight variables to analyze the user dependence on digital tools.

Table 4.57 Digital Tools Dependence

S.No	Description	No Dependence		Rare Dependence		Occasional		Frequently		Mean	Std.	Rank
1	To send email to utilise library services	77	3.7%	126	6.1%	663	32.2%	1191	57.9%	3.44	.771	1
2	University campus is Wi-Fi enabled	49	2.4%	313	15.2%	1552	75.4%	143	7.0%	2.87	.548	4
3	Online book reservation and renewal	77	3.7%	629	30.6%	1333	64.8%	18	.9%	2.63	.571	7
4	High speed internet access facilities	40	1.9%	398	19.3%	1037	50.4%	582	28.3%	3.05	.743	3
5	Web OPAC	92	4.5%	762	37.0%	1203	58.5%	0	.0%	2.54	.581	8
6	Digital notice board	45	2.2%	552	26.8%	1293	62.9%	167	8.1%	2.77	.620	5
7	Plasma TV	31	1.5%	681	33.1%	1335	64.9%	10	.5%	2.64	.519	6
8	Printing and scanning facility	75	3.6%	222	10.8%	907	44.1%	853	41.5%	3.23	.784	2

Table 4.57 shows that the users are more dependent on email to utilize library services. Printing and scanning facilities was indicated as second and high speed internet access facilities as third preference. Mean varies from 3.44 and 2.54 which indicate that the responses lie between occasional and frequent. Standard deviation ranges from 0.519 to 0.784 and this demotes there is no significant difference between the opinion of respondents. The study was further extended to the type of university.

Table 4.58 Digital Tools Dependence Vs Type of University

S.	Description	Central University			State University			Deemed University			Total		
No		Mean	Std.	Rank	Mean	Std.	Rank	Mean	Std.	Rank	Mean	Std.	Rank
1	To send email to utilise library services	3.04	.855	3	3.15	.952	2	3.67	.525	1	3.44	.771	1
2	University campus is Wi-Fi enabled	3.31	1.132	2	2.83	.447	4	2.82	.408	8	2.87	.548	4
3	Online book reservation and renewal	2.52	.605	6	2.29	.653	7	2.83	.397	4	2.63	.571	7
4	High speed internet access facilities	2.58	.650	5	2.93	.584	3	3.19	.792	3	3.05	.743	3
5	Web OPAC	1.90	.299	8	2.19	.586	8	2.83	.397	4	2.54	.581	8
6	Digital notice board	3.48	.752	1	2.45	.698	5	2.83	.397	4	2.77	.620	5
7	Plasma TV	2.29	.714	7	2.40	.494	6	2.83	.397	4	2.64	.519	6
8	Printing and scanning facility	2.82	.892	4	3.22	.797	1	3.30	.737	2	3.23	.784	2

Table 4.58 shows that the users from central university have indicated digital notice board as first preference followed by Wi-Fi enabled campus and email to utilize library services. State university respondents have indicated printing and scanning facility as their top preference followed by email facility for library services and high speed internet access facility. Respondents from deemed university have indicated their first preference as sending email for utilizing library services. Printing and scanning facilities was indicated as second and high speed internet access facilities as third preference. The order of preference varies with the type of university. The study was extended to category of user.

Table 4.59 Digital Tools Dependence Vs Category of User

S.No	Description	Research Scholars			Faculty Members			Total		
		Mean	Std.	Rank	Mean	Std.	Rank	Mean	Std.	Rank
1	To send email to utilise library services	3.45	.789	1	3.41	.726	1	3.44	.771	1
2	University campus is Wi-Fi enabled	2.86	.547	4	2.89	.549	4	2.87	.548	4
3	Online book reservation and renewal	2.62	.581	7	2.64	.547	7	2.63	.571	7
4	High speed internet access facilities	3.05	.751	3	3.04	.725	3	3.05	.743	3
5	Web OPAC	2.54	.589	8	2.55	.563	8	2.54	.581	8
6	Digital notice board	2.77	.625	5	2.77	.608	5	2.77	.620	5
7	Plasma TV	2.64	.521	6	2.65	.515	6	2.64	.519	6
8	Printing and scanning facility	3.22	.786	2	3.27	.778	2	3.23	.784	2

Table 4.59 shows that both the categories of respondents have indicated their first preference as sending email for utilizing library services. Printing and scanning facilities was indicated as second and high speed internet access facilities as third preference. All the preferences were indicated uniformly. The study was extended to gender of the respondents.

Table 4.60 Digital Tools Dependence Vs Gender

S. No	Description	Male			Female			Total		
		Mean	Std.	Rank	Mean	Std.	Rank	Mean	Std.	Rank
1	To send email to utilise library services	3.45	.776	1	3.42	.760	1	3.44	.771	1
2	University campus is Wi-Fi enabled	2.86	.520	4	2.89	.604	4	2.87	.548	4
3	Online book reservation and renewal	2.62	.579	7	2.64	.553	6	2.63	.571	7
4	High speed internet access facilities	3.07	.764	3	3.00	.693	3	3.05	.743	3
5	Web OPAC	2.55	.583	8	2.51	.578	8	2.54	.581	8
6	Digital notice board	2.75	.616	5	2.81	.626	5	2.77	.620	5
7	Plasma TV	2.65	.518	6	2.62	.522	7	2.64	.519	6
8	Printing and scanning facility	3.22	.779	2	3.25	.795	2	3.23	.784	2

Table 4.60 shows that gender of respondent has no differentiation on their opinion on the order of preference. Respondents have indicated their first preference as sending email for utilizing library services. Printing and scanning facilities was indicated as second and high speed internet access facilities as third preference.

Table 4.61 Digital Tools Dependence – Overall Rank

S. No	Description	Overall	Central University	State University	Deemed University	Research Scholars	Faculty Members	Male	Female
1	To send email to utilise library services	1	3	2	1	1	1	1	1
2	University campus is Wi-Fi enabled	4	2	4	8	4	4	4	4
3	Online book reservation and renewal	7	6	7	4	7	7	7	6
4	High speed internet access facilities	3	5	3	3	3	3	3	3
5	Web OPAC	8	8	8	4	8	8	8	8
6	Digital notice board	5	1	5	4	5	5	5	5
7	Plasma TV	6	7	6	4	6	6	6	7
8	Printing and scanning facility	2	4	1	2	2	2	2	2

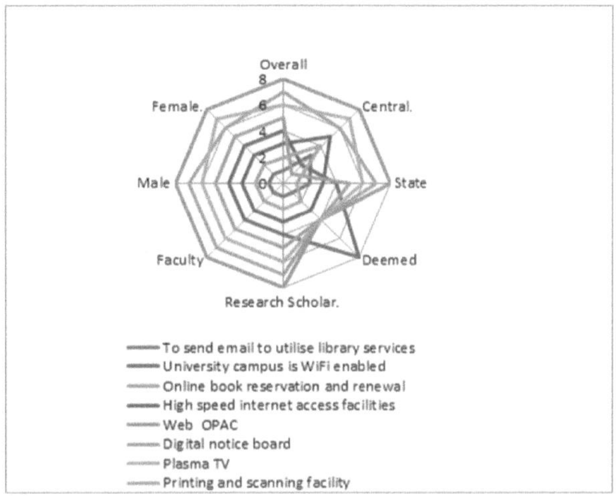

Figure 4.20 : Digital Tools Dependence – Overall Rank

From Table 4.61 and Figure 4.20, it can be seen that the preferences were uniform among the other categories except different type of universities. Most of the respondents have indicated that library facilities should be utilized by sending mails.

4.6.5 Digital Service Provides

In Table 4.62, dependence on digital service providers in five scales namely "no dependence", "rare dependence", "occasional", "frequently" and high dependence. Mean and standard deviation was calculated and the appropriate ranks were assigned for the nine variables to analyze the user dependence on digital service providers.

Table 4.62 Digital Service Providers Dependence

S. No	Description	No Dependence		Rare Dependence		Occasional		Frequently		High		Mean	Std.	Rank
1	Study material through web portal	88	4.3%	175	8.5%	690	33.5%	1015	49.3%	89	4.3%	3.41	.869	4
2	National Knowledge Network (NKN)	122	5.9%	179	8.7%	920	44.7%	510	24.8%	326	15.8%	3.36	1.038	6
3	Spoken Tutorial IIT Bombay	156	7.6%	301	14.6%	728	35.4%	828	40.3%	44	2.1%	3.15	.957	7
4	Networking facilities	16	.8%	131	6.4%	302	14.7%	918	44.6%	690	33.5%	4.04	.898	1
5	Open Access Knowledge Resources Material	35	1.7%	183	8.9%	617	30.0%	861	41.9%	361	17.5%	3.65	.927	3
6	Federated Search Engine Facilities	7	.3%	678	33.0%	740	36.0%	632	30.7%	0	.0%	2.97	.806	9
7	SMS alert service	27	1.3%	116	5.6%	342	16.6%	1060	51.5%	512	24.9%	3.93	.869	2
8	Social Network Services	61	3.0%	306	14.9%	648	31.5%	859	41.8%	183	8.9%	3.39	.944	5
9	E-Mail Management	13	.6%	605	29.4%	614	29.8%	769	37.4%	56	2.7%	3.12	.888	8

From ***Table 4.62,*** it can be inferred that the networking facilities were more depended on. Second and third preference was indicated as SMS alert service and open access knowledge resources. Least preference was indicated as federated search engine facilities. Mean varies from 4.04 and 2.97 which indicate that the responses lie between the high dependence and occasional dependence. Standard deviation lies between 0.806 and 1.038 which indicates that there exists no significant difference between the responses. The study was further analysed with the type of university the respondents affiliated to.

Table 4.63 Digital Service Providers Dependence Vs Type of University

S. No	Description	Central University			State University			Deemed University			Total		
		Mean	Std.	Rank	Mean	Std.	Rank	Mean	Std.	Rank	Mean	Std.	Rank
1	Study material through web portal	2.64	.927	8	3.31	1.002	5	3.59	.687	5	3.41	.869	4
2	National knowledge network (NKN)	3.14	1.009	5	2.94	.654	6	3.63	1.126	4	3.36	1.038	6
3	Spoken Tutorial IIT Bombay	3.17	.896	4	2.60	.822	8	3.44	.904	6	3.15	.957	7
4	Networking facilities	3.56	1.285	1	3.91	.850	1	4.18	.808	2	4.04	.898	1
5	Open Access Knowledge Resources Material	3.26	.546	3	3.50	.793	4	3.79	1.011	3	3.65	.927	3
6	Federated Search Engine Facilities	2.36	.553	9	2.51	.653	9	3.32	.730	8	2.97	.806	9
7	SMS alert service	2.98	.889	6	3.75	.785	2	4.18	.777	1	3.93	.869	2
8	Social Network Services	2.90	.979	7	3.51	.643	3	3.40	1.047	7	3.39	.944	5
9	E-Mail Management	3.34	1.005	2	2.72	.941	7	3.31	.753	9	3.12	.888	8

From ***Table 4.63,*** it can be inferred that the networking facilities were more depended by respondents from Central and State Universities. Deemed University respondents have indicated that SMS alert service as their first preference. Second and third preferences vary with the type of university. Least preference was indicated as federated search engine facilities except respondents from Deemed University and they have indicated email management as their least preference. The study was further analysed with the category of the respondent.

Table 4.64 Digital Service Providers Dependence Vs Category of User

S. No	Description	Research Scholars			Faculty Members			Total		
		Mean	Std.	Rank	Mean	Std.	Rank	Mean	Std.	Rank
1	Study material through web portal	3.40	.877	4	3.44	.850	4	3.41	.869	4
2	National Knowledge Network (NKN)	3.40	1.070	5	3.25	.952	6	3.36	1.038	6
3	Spoken Tutorial IIT Bombay	3.16	.976	7	3.12	.912	7	3.15	.957	7
4	Networking facilities	4.03	.909	1	4.05	.872	1	4.04	.898	1
5	Open Access Knowledge Resources Material	3.67	.943	3	3.60	.889	3	3.65	.927	3
6	Federated Search Engine Facilities	2.97	.803	9	2.97	.815	9	2.97	.806	9
7	SMS alert service	3.94	.876	2	3.90	.850	2	3.93	.869	2
8	Social Network Services	3.39	.964	6	3.39	.895	5	3.39	.944	5
9	E-Mail Management	3.12	.888	8	3.11	.886	8	3.12	.888	8

All the preferences were uniformly indicated by the respondents without any difference in respect to their category. From Table 4.64, it can be inferred that the networking facilities were more depended by respondents followed by SMS alert service and open access knowledge resources material. Least preference was indicated as federated search engine facilities. The study was further analyzed on gender of the respondent.

Table 4.65 Digital Service Providers Dependence Vs Gender

S.No	Description	Male			Female			Total		
		Mean	Std.	Rank	Mean	Std.	Rank	Mean	Std.	Rank
1	Study material through web portal	3.42	.882	4	3.39	.841	4	3.41	.869	4
2	National Knowledge Network (NKN)	3.38	1.048	6	3.31	1.016	6	3.36	1.038	6
3	Spoken Tutorial IIT Bombay	3.17	.955	7	3.10	.961	8	3.15	.957	7
4	Networking facilities	4.07	.914	1	3.98	.859	1	4.04	.898	1
5	Open Access Knowledge Resources Material	3.69	.943	3	3.55	.885	3	3.65	.927	3
6	Federated Search Engine Facilities	2.99	.812	9	2.93	.792	9	2.97	.806	9
7	SMS alert service	3.99	.863	2	3.80	.868	2	3.93	.869	2
8	Social Network Services	3.41	.972	5	3.34	.879	5	3.39	.944	5
9	E-Mail Management	3.12	.888	8	3.12	.888	7	3.12	.888	8

From ***Table 4.65,*** it can be inferred that the networking facilities were more depended by respondents followed by SMS alert service and open access knowledge resources material. Least preference was indicated as federated search engine facilities. There is no difference in the order of preference among the respondents based on their gender.

Table 4.66 Digital Service Providers Dependence Vs Overall Rank

S. No	Description	Overall	Central University	State University	Deemed University	Research Scholars	Faculty Members	Male	Female
1	Study material through web portal	4	8	5	5	4	4	4	4
2	National Knowledge Network (NKN)	6	5	6	4	5	6	6	6
3	Spoken Tutorial IIT Bombay	7	4	8	6	7	7	7	8
4	Networking facilities	1	1	1	2	1	1	1	1
5	Open Access Knowledge Resources Material	3	3	4	3	3	3	4	3
6	Federated Search Engine Facilities	9	9	9	8	9	9	9	9
7	SMS alert service	2	6	2	1	2	2	2	2
8	Social Network Services	5	7	3	7	6	5	5	5
9	E-Mail Management	8	2	7	9	8	8	8	7

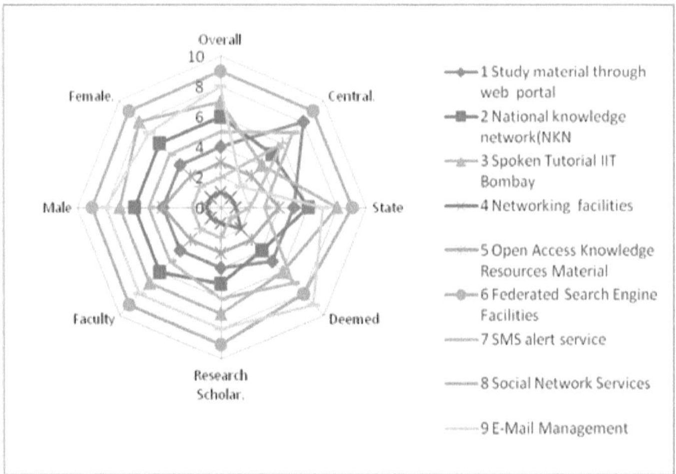

Figure 4.21 Digital Service Providers Dependence Vs Overall Rank

From Table 4.66 ad Figure 4.21, it can be inference that there is no difference in the order of preference among the respondents based on their gender or category of the respondent. But there is a slight variation between the opinions with respect to the type of university they are affiliated to.

4.6.6 Digital Service Policy Dependence

In Table 4.67, dependence on digital service policy in five scales namely "no dependence", "rare dependence", "occasional", "frequently" and high dependence. Mean and standard deviation was calculated and the appropriate ranks were assigned for the eleven variables to analyze the user dependence on digital service policy.

Table 4.67 Digital Service Policy Dependence

S. No	Description	No Dependence		Rare Dependence		Occasional		Frequently		High		Mean	Std.	Rank
1	Citation analysis	669	32.5%	558	27.1%	394	19.2%	416	20.2%	20	1.0%	2.30	1.151	4
2	Digital Reference service	180	8.8%	344	16.7%	782	38.0%	747	36.3%	4	.2%	3.02	.942	2
3	Anti-Plagiarism service	904	43.9%	320	15.6%	390	19.0%	422	20.5%	21	1.0%	2.19	1.227	7
4	Digital Copy rights Issue service	782	38.0%	527	25.6%	365	17.7%	361	17.5%	22	1.1%	2.18	1.151	8
5	Google scholar uploading service	949	46.1%	286	13.9%	390	19.0%	411	20.0%	21	1.0%	2.16	1.232	9
6	Research Gate uploading service	1045	50.8%	236	11.5%	365	17.7%	391	19.0%	20	1.0%	2.08	1.236	11
7	INFLIBNET Vidwan	940	45.7%	371	18.0%	306	14.9%	430	20.9%	10	.5%	2.12	1.213	10
8	IMPACT FACTOR, H-Index, Calculating service	754	36.7%	576	28.0%	316	15.4%	399	19.4%	12	.6%	2.19	1.145	6
9	Scholarly information	736	35.8%	549	26.7%	324	15.8%	436	21.2%	12	.6%	2.24	1.165	5
10	Conference alert services	29	1.4%	456	22.2%	1438	69.9%	120	5.8%	14	.7%	2.82	.576	3
11	Commercial Reference Management Tools and services	173	8.4%	322	15.7%	790	38.4%	752	36.6%	20	1.0%	3.06	.946	1

From ***Table 4.67,*** it can be inferred that commercial reference management tools and services was indicated as first preference followed by digital reference service and conference alert services. Mean ranges from 3.06 and 2.08 which indicate that the responses lie between occasional and frequent dependence. Standard deviation lies between 0.576 and 1.236 and it can be inferred that there is no significant difference between the respondents. The study was further extended to type of university.

Table 4.68 Digital Service Policy Dependence Vs Type of University

S.	Description	Central University			State University			Deemed University			Total		
No		Mean	Std.	Rank	Mean	Std.	Rank	Mean	Std.	Rank	Mean	Std.	Rank
1	Citation analysis	1.67	.961	7	2.26	1.156	4	2.42	1.142	4	2.30	1.151	4
2	Digital Reference service	2.95	.967	2	3.02	.939	2	3.04	.941	2	3.02	.942	2
3	Anti-Plagiarism service	1.47	.976	10	2.05	1.199	7	2.38	1.226	7	2.19	1.227	7
4	Digital Copy rights Issue service	1.29	.456	11	2.01	1.142	9	2.41	1.148	6	2.18	1.151	8
5	Google scholar uploading service	1.67	1.164	9	2.03	1.241	8	2.31	1.209	10	2.16	1.232	9
6	Research Gate uploading service	1.67	1.149	8	1.91	1.184	10	2.24	1.252	11	2.08	1.236	11
7	INFLIBNET Vidwan	1.76	1.182	4	1.70	.995	11	2.42	1.241	5	2.12	1.213	10
8	IMPACT FACTOR, H-Index, Calculating service	1.70	.955	6	2.05	1.119	6	2.35	1.156	8	2.19	1.145	6
9	Scholarly information	1.74	.945	5	2.19	1.152	5	2.35	1.183	9	2.24	1.165	5
10	Conference alert services	2.76	.466	3	2.81	.604	3	2.84	.576	3	2.82	.576	3
11	Commercial Reference Management Tools and services	3.04	1.038	1	3.09	.946	1	3.04	.930	1	3.06	.946	1

From T*able 4.68,* it can be inferred that the commercial reference management tools and services were more depended by respondents followed by digital reference services and conference alert service uniformly by respondents from all type of university. Least preference was indicated as digital copy rights issue service by Central University respondents, INFLIBNET Vidwan by State University respondents and Research gate uploading service by Deemed University respondents. The study was further analysed with the category of the respondent.

Table 4.69 Digital Service Policy Dependence Vs Category of User

S.No	Description	Research Scholars			Faculty Members			Total		
		Mean	Std.	Rank	Mean	Std.	Rank	Mean	Std.	Rank
1	Citation analysis	2.31	1.150	4	2.28	1.152	5	2.30	1.151	4
2	Digital Reference service	3.04	.935	2	2.99	.958	2	3.02	.942	2
3	Anti-Plagiarism service	2.20	1.222	6	2.18	1.239	8	2.19	1.227	7
4	Digital Copy rights Issue service	2.18	1.149	8	2.18	1.156	7	2.18	1.151	8
5	Google scholar uploading service	2.18	1.236	9	2.12	1.222	9	2.16	1.232	9
6	Research Gate uploading service	2.09	1.238	11	2.04	1.231	11	2.08	1.236	11
7	INFLIBNET Vidwan	2.14	1.213	10	2.10	1.213	10	2.12	1.213	10
8	IMPACT ACTOR, H-Index, Calculating service	2.18	1.140	7	2.23	1.158	6	2.19	1.145	6
9	Scholarly information	2.22	1.159	5	2.29	1.181	4	2.24	1.165	5
10	Conference alert services	2.83	.576	3	2.80	.578	3	2.82	.576	3
11	Commercial Reference Management Tools and services	3.07	.933	1	3.04	.976	1	3.06	.946	1

All the preferences were uniformly indicated by the respondents without any difference in respect to their category. From Table 4.69, it can be inferred that commercial reference management tools and services were more depended by respondents followed by digital reference service and conference alert service. Least preference was indicated as Research gate uploading service. The study was further analyzed on gender of the respondent.

Table 4.70 Digital Service Policy Dependence Vs Gender

S.No	Description	Male			Female			Total		
		Mean	**Std.**	**Rank**	**Mean**	**Std.**	**Rank**	**Mean**	**Std.**	**Rank**
1	Citation analysis	2.36	1.162	4	2.17	1.115	4	2.30	1.151	4
2	Digital Reference service	3.02	.935	2	3.04	.959	2	3.02	.942	2
3	Anti-Plagiarism service	2.23	1.238	8	2.10	1.199	7	2.19	1.227	7
4	Digital Copy rights Issue service	2.23	1.159	7	2.08	1.127	8	2.18	1.151	8
5	Google scholar uploading service	2.20	1.233	8	2.07	1.225	9	2.16	1.232	9
6	Research Gate uploading service	2.12	1.256	11	2.00	1.189	11	2.08	1.236	11
7	INFLIBNET Vidwan	2.18	1.225	10	2.01	1.179	10	2.12	1.213	10
8	IMPACT FACTOR, H-Index, Calculating service	2.23	1.153	6	2.12	1.127	6	2.19	1.145	6
9	Scholarly information	2.28	1.182	5	2.15	1.125	5	2.24	1.165	5
10	Conference alert services	2.82	.582	3	2.82	.565	3	2.82	.576	3
11	Commercial Reference Management Tools and services	3.06	.943	1	3.07	.952	1	3.06	.946	1

From ***Table 4.70,*** it can be inferred that commercial reference management tools and services were more depended by respondents followed by digital reference service and conference alert service. Least preference was indicated as Research Gate uploading service. There is no difference in the order of preference among the respondents based on their gender.

Table 4.71 Digital Service Policy Dependence – Overall Rank

S. No	Description	Overall	Central University	State University	Deemed University	Research Scholars	Faculty Members	Male	Female
1	Citation analysis	4	7	4	4	4	5	4	4
2	Digital Reference service	2	2	2	2	2	2	2	2
3	Anti-Plagiarism service	7	10	7	7	6	8	8	7
4	Digital Copy rights Issue service	8	11	9	6	8	7	7	8
5	Google scholar uploading service	9	9	8	10	9	9	8	9
6	Research Gate uploading service	11	8	10	11	11	11	11	11
7	INFLIBNET Vidwan	10	4	11	5	10	10	10	10
8	IMPACT FACTOR, H-Index, Calculating service	6	6	6	8	7	6	6	6
9	Scholarly information	5	5	5	9	5	4	5	5
10	Conference alert services	3	3	3	3	3	3	3	3
11	Commercial Reference Management Tools and services	1	1	1	1	1	1	1	1

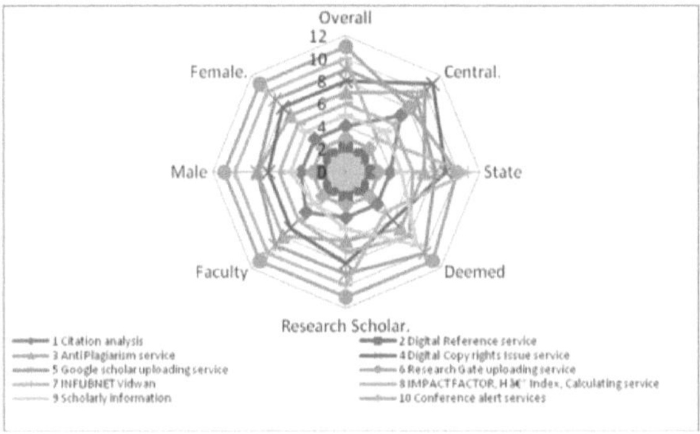

Figure 4.22 Digital Service Policy Dependence – Overall Rank

From Table 4.71 and Figure 4.22, it can be inferred that there is no difference in the order of preference among the respondents based on their gender or category of the respondent. But there is a slight variation between the opinions with respect to the type of university they are affiliated to.

4.7 LIMITATION

4.7.1 Limitation of Information

Limitation of information from web search was contented by the users and it can be inferred from Table 4.72 and Figure 4.22 that they benefited to large extent from web search. Around 65 % of the respondents have indicated that they get information from web search. Around 30% of the respondents have indicated that the very little information was got from web search, and 5% have indicated that could not get any relevant information from web search. Three variables were analyzed to ascertain the opinion on digital services and comparison with traditional and convention libraries. Number of respondents and its percentage are tabulated in Table 4.73.

Table 4.72 Obtain the information from Web-Search

S. No	Description	Count	%
1	Not at all	105	5.1%
2	Very little extent	610	29.7%
3	Some Extent	84	4.1%
4	Large Extent	1237	60.1%
5	Very Large Extent	21	1.0%

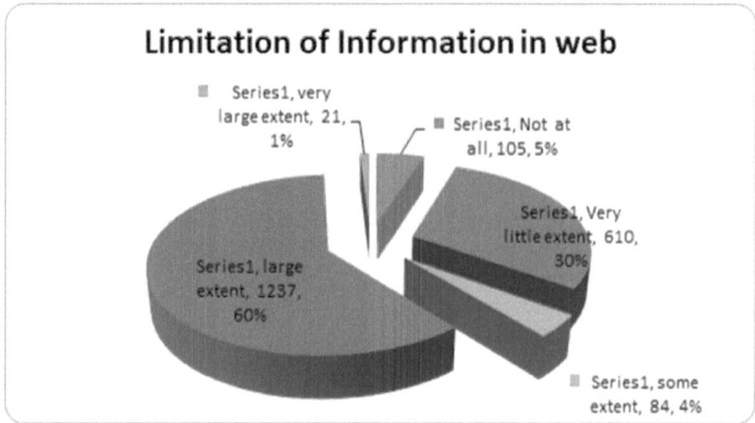

Figure 4.23 Obtain the information from Web-Search

Table 4.73 Obtain the information from Web-Search

S.No	Description	Agree		Disagree	
1	Use various digital Library Services on a payment basis	1249	60.7%	808	39.3%
2	Traditional Libraries will be replaced by Digital Libraries in the near future	1302	63.3%	755	36.7%
3	Digital Libraries can provide better services than the Conventional Library services	1030	50.1%	1027	49.9%

From Table 4.73, it can be inferred that the respondents utilize various digital library services on a payment basis (60.7%), believe that the digital libraries will replace traditional libraries in the near future (63.3%) and digital libraries can provide better services that the conventional library services (50.1%).

4.7.2 Digital Environment Advantages

Advantages of digital environment were ascertained with eight variables on five scales namely "not at all", "very little extent", "some extent", "large extent" and "very large extent". Mean and standard deviation was calculated and ranks were assigned based on mean and standard deviation.

Table 4.74 Digital Environment Advantages

S. No	Description	Not at all		Very little extent		Some Extent		Large Extent		Very Large Extent		Mean	Std.	Rank
1	We can save more physical space.	178	8.7%	476	23.1%	289	14.0%	529	25.7%	585	28.4%	3.42	1.340	1
2	Library services shifted from 'just in case' to 'just in time'	589	28.6%	603	29.3%	283	13.8%	518	25.2%	64	3.1%	2.45	1.229	8
3	You can access from anywhere in anytime.	179	8.7%	300	14.6%	287	14.0%	1215	59.1%	76	3.7%	3.34	1.056	2
4	Availability of information to all users simultaneously	162	7.9%	350	17.0%	950	46.2%	543	26.4%	52	2.5%	2.99	.922	5
5	Easy retrieval	167	8.1%	374	18.2%	637	31.0%	823	40.0%	56	2.7%	3.11	1.002	3
6	No maintenance	171	8.3%	297	14.4%	844	41.0%	686	33.3%	59	2.9%	3.08	.959	4
7	Enables networking of various internal resources	168	8.2%	460	22.4%	889	43.2%	482	23.4%	58	2.8%	2.90	.943	6
8	Networking of other libraries	190	9.2%	461	22.4%	840	40.8%	508	24.7%	58	2.8%	2.89	.971	7

Table 4.74 indicates that the respondents were very keen that they can save more physical space, followed by anywhere/ anytime access and easy retrieval of information with search and retrieval tools. Mean ranges between 2.45 and 3.42 and this indicates that the respondents have indicated that they depend on digital library environment from some extent to large extent. Standard deviation lies between 0.922 and 1.340 which indicates that there is no significant difference between the respondents. The study was further extended to the type of university.

Table 4.75 Digital Environment Advantages Vs Type of University

S. No	Description	Central University			State University			Deemed University			Total		
		Mean	Std.	Rank	Mean	Std.	Rank	Mean	Std.	Rank	Mean	Std.	Rank
1	We can save more physical space.	3.43	1.276	1	3.47	1.354	2	3.39	1.342	1	3.42	1.340	1
2	Library services shifted from 'just in case' to 'just in time'	2.55	1.252	8	2.38	1.232	8	2.47	1.223	8	2.45	1.229	8
3	You can access from anywhere in anytime.	3.40	1.135	2	3.49	.984	1	3.25	1.071	2	3.34	1.056	2
4	Availability of information to all users simultaneously	2.95	.885	5	3.01	.899	5	2.98	.941	5	2.99	.922	5
5	Easy retrieval	3.06	1.054	3	3.07	.956	4	3.14	1.018	3	3.11	1.002	3
6	No maintenance	3.02	1.125	4	3.10	.910	3	3.08	.956	4	3.08	.959	4
7	Enables networking of various internal resources	2.89	1.032	6	2.82	.983	7	2.95	.902	6	2.90	.943	6
8	Networking of other libraries	2.80	1.117	7	2.84	1.020	6	2.94	.915	7	2.89	.971	7

Table 4.75 indicates that the respondents from Central and Deemed Universities were very keen that they can save more physical space, followed by anywhere/anytime access and easy retrieval of information with search and retrieval tools. Least preference was indicated uniformly as Library services shifted from 'just in case' to 'just in time'. Respondents from state have indicated the same variables. The study was further extended to the category of user.

Table 4.76 Digital Service Policy Dependence Vs Category of User

S.No	Description	Research Scholars			Faculty Members			Total		
		Mean	Std.	Rank	Mean	Std.	Rank	Mean	Std.	Rank
1	We can save more physical space.	3.43	1.328	1	3.40	1.368	1	3.42	1.340	1
2	Library services shifted from 'just in case' to 'just in time'	2.48	1.236	8	2.38	1.213	8	2.45	1.229	8
3	You can access from anywhere in anytime.	3.34	1.060	2	3.36	1.046	2	3.34	1.056	2
4	Availability of information to all users simultaneously	3.00	.919	5	2.96	.929	5	2.99	.922	5
5	Easy retrieval	3.15	.985	3	3.03	1.037	3	3.11	1.002	3
6	No maintenance	3.11	.947	4	3.02	.983	4	3.08	.959	4
7	Enables networking of various internal resources	2.91	.932	7	2.88	.968	6	2.90	.943	6
8	Networking of other libraries	2.92	.960	6	2.84	.995	7	2.89	.971	7

Table 4.76 indicates that research scholars and faculty members were very keen that they can save more physical space, followed by anywhere/anytime access and easy retrieval of information with search and retrieval tools. Least preference was indicated as Library services shifted from 'just in case' to 'just in time' by all categories of respondents invariably. The study was further extended to the gender of the respondent.

Table 4.77 Digital Service Policy Dependence Vs Gender

S.No	Description	Male			Female			Total		
		Mean	Std.	Rank	Mean	Std.	Rank	Mean	Std.	Rank
1	We can save more physical space.	3.44	1.330	1	3.37	1.361	1	3.42	1.340	1
2	Library services shifted from 'just in case' to 'just in time'	2.45	1.232	8	2.44	1.223	8	2.45	1.229	8
3	You can access from anywhere in anytime.	3.36	1.067	2	3.31	1.030	2	3.34	1.056	2
4	Availability of information to all users simultaneously	2.98	.940	5	3.00	.883	5	2.99	.922	5
5	Easy retrieval	3.13	.999	3	3.06	1.008	4	3.11	1.002	3
6	No maintenance	3.08	.961	4	3.08	.953	3	3.08	.959	4
7	Enables networking of various internal resources	2.89	.952	6	2.94	.923	6	2.90	.943	6
8	Networking of other libraries	2.89	.970	7	2.90	.973	7	2.89	.971	7

Table 4.77 indicates that all the respondents have prioritized to save more physical space, followed by anywhere/anytime access. Easy retrieval of information was indicated as third preference by male respondents and maintenance free environment was indicated as third preference by female respondents. Least preference was indicated as Library services shifted from 'just in case' to 'just in time' by all respondents without gender bias. The study was further extended to the gender of the respondent.

Table 4.78 Digital Service Policy Dependence – Overall Rank

S. No	Description	Overall	Central University	State University	Deemed University	Research Scholars	Faculty Members	Male	Female
1	We can save more physical space	1	1	2	1	1	1	1	1
2	Library services shifted from 'just in case' to 'just in time'	8	8	8	8	8	8	8	8
3	You can access from anywhere in anytime.	2	2	1	2	2	2	2	2
4	Availability of information to all users simultaneously	5	5	5	5	5	5	5	5
5	Easy retrieval	3	3	4	3	3	3	3	4
6	No maintenance	4	4	3	4	4	4	4	3
7	Enables networking of various internal resources	6	6	7	6	7	6	6	6
8	Networking of other libraries	7	7	6	7	6	7	7	7

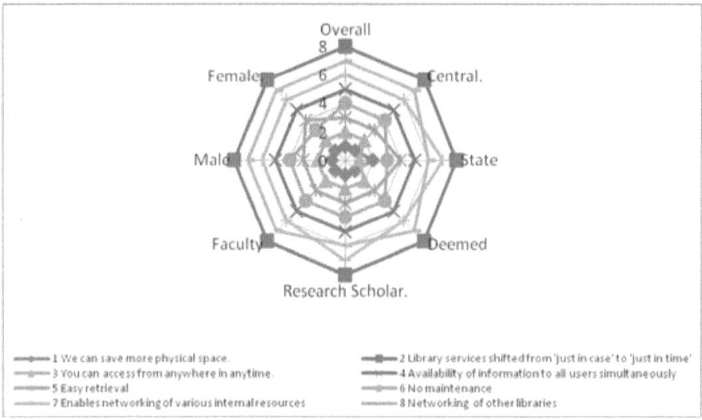

Figure 4.24 Digital Service Policy Dependence – Overall Rank

From Table 4.78 ad Figure 4.24, it can be inferred that there is no difference in the order of preference among the respondents based on their gender or category of the respondent.

Further hierarchical cluster test has also been administrated to identify the group of variables of digital service policy that are to be considered immediately. The dendrogram thus arrived has been shown in Figure 4.25.

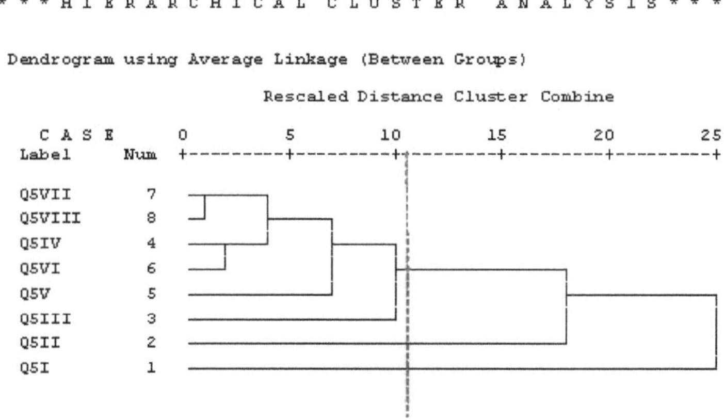

Figure 4.25 Digital Service Policy Dependence - Cluster analysis

It can be seen from Figure 4.25 that there exist three major clusters derived from the eight variables. At 42% level, three clusters were formed. Cluster I comprises of one variable "save more physical space". Similarly cluster II comprises of one variable "Library services shifted from 'just in case' to 'just in time'". Cluster I and Cluster II can be named together as Auxiliary digital policy. Cluster III comprises of six variables such as "One can access from anywhere in anytime", "Easy retrieval", "No maintenance", "Availability of information to all users simultaneously", "Networking of other libraries" and "Enables networking of various internal resources". This cluster can be named as Primary digital policy.

In order to identify the relation between variables, proximity analysis was administrated. The proximity matrix analysis will enable to identify the nearest and farthest variables. The proximity matrix has been employed for the digital service policy variables and the same is shown in Table 4.79.

Table 4.79 Digital Service Policy – Proximity Matrix

S. No	Description	1	2	3	4	5	6	7	8
1	We can save more physical space.	.000							
2	Library services shifted from 'just in case' to 'just in time'	9734.000	.000						
3	You can access from anywhere in anytime.	5068.000	6620.000	.000					
4	Availability of information to all users simultaneously	4990.000	4268.000	3300.000	.000				
5	Easy retrieval	5386.000	5122.000	2888.000	2438.000	.000			
6	No maintenance	5066.000	4784.000	2758.000	1796.000	2218.000	.000		
7	Enables networking of various internal resources	5813.000	3943.000	3441.000	2235.000	2769.000	1581.000	.000	
8	Networking of other libraries	5934.000	3642.000	3732.000	2404.000	3280.000	2322.000	1535.000	.000

The proximity matrix Tables 4.79 enables to identify the closely associated variables and distinctly associated variables. The closely associated variables and distinctly associated variables are shown below.

Closely associated variables

- Networking of other libraries and Enables networking of various internal resources.
- Enables networking of various internal resources and No maintenance.
- No maintenance and availability of information to all users simultaneously.

Distinctly associated variables

- "Just in case and just in time" and "Save more Physical Space".
- "Access from anywhere in any time" and "Just in case and just in time".
- "Enables networking of various internal resources" and "save more physical space".
- "Networking of other libraries" and "saves more physical space".

4.7.3 Digital Environment Barriers

Eight variables were identified to ascertain the barriers to digital environment on five scales namely "not at all", "very little extent", "some extent", "large extent" and "very large extent". Mean and standard deviation was calculated and ranks were assigned based on mean and standard deviation.

Table 4.80 Digital Environment Barriers

S. No	Description	Not at all		Very little extent		Some Extent		Large Extent		Very Large Extent		Mean	Std.	Rank
1	More complex than the existing library system	163	7.9%	747	36.3%	830	40.4%	247	12.0%	70	3.4%	2.67	.909	5
2	Needs training for the users to use digital library services	118	5.7%	565	27.5%	985	47.9%	331	16.1%	58	2.8%	2.83	.865	4
3	Requires more investment on creation of digital libraries	139	6.8%	279	13.6%	1297	63.1%	276	13.4%	66	3.2%	2.93	.815	1
4	Requires frequent up gradation of hardware and software	135	6.6%	399	19.4%	1089	52.9%	383	18.6%	51	2.5%	2.91	.857	3
5	Non-existing of ownership of digital resources	141	6.9%	320	15.6%	1216	59.1%	327	15.9%	53	2.6%	2.92	.828	2

S. No	Description	Not at all		Very little extent		Some Extent		Large Extent		Very Large Extent		Mean	Std.	Rank
6	Making existing staff services redundant	820	39.9%	725	35.2%	172	8.4%	280	13.6%	60	2.9%	2.04	1.135	8
7	Digital Libraries cut down various personal or personalized services drastically.	758	36.8%	791	38.5%	172	8.4%	280	13.6%	56	2.7%	2.07	1.112	7
8	Transactions will become machine to man rather than man to man	524	25.5%	1038	50.5%	167	8.1%	272	13.2%	56	2.7%	2.17	1.040	6

Table 4.80 shows that the respondents have indicated the important barrier as library requires more investment on creation of digital libraries followed by non-existing of ownership of digital resources and requires frequent up gradation of hardware and software. Mean ranges between 2.04 and 2.93 and this indicates that the respondents consider making existing staff services redundant. Standard deviation lies between 0.922 and 1.340 which indicates that there is no significant difference between the respondents. The study was further extended to the type of university.

Table 4.81 Digital Environment Barriers Vs Type of University

S.	Description	Central University			State University			Deemed University			Total		
No		Mean	Std.	Rank	Mean	Std.	Rank	Mean	Std.	Rank	Mean	Std.	Rank
1	More complex than the existing library system	2.76	1.205	4	2.69	.586	4	2.64	.995	5	2.67	.909	5
2	Needs training for the users to use digital library services	3.11	.879	1	2.55	.685	5	2.93	.913	2	2.83	.865	4
3	Requires more investment on creation of digital libraries	2.79	1.024	3	2.94	.430	1	2.94	.929	1	2.93	.815	1
4	Requires frequent up gradation of hardware and software	2.71	1.026	5	2.93	.448	3	2.93	.985	3	2.91	.857	3
5	Non-existing of ownership of digital resources	2.80	1.011	2	2.94	.432	2	2.92	.951	4	2.92	.828	2
6	Making existing staff services redundant	2.13	1.257	7	1.55	.774	8	2.30	1.193	8	2.04	1.135	8

S. No	Description	Central University			State University			Deemed University			Total		
		Mean	Std.	Rank	Mean	Std.	Rank	Mean	Std.	Rank	Mean	Std.	Rank
7	Digital Libraries cut down various personal or personalized services drastically.	2.07	1.286	8	1.61	.768	7	2.32	1.160	7	2.07	1.112	7
8	Transactions will become machine to man rather than man to man	2.35	1.116	6	1.76	.719	6	2.37	1.107	6	2.17	1.040	6

Table 4.81 indicates that the respondents from State and Deemed Universities felt that digital library requires frequent up gradation of hardware and software as the most important barrier. Central university respondents have indicated training for the users to use digital library services is needed utmost. Second preference of Central and State Universities respondent were non-existing of ownership of digital resources, whereas Deemed University needs to have training for the users to use Digital Knowledge Management and library services.

Third preference of Central University respondents was indicated as requires more investment on creation of digital libraries. State and Deemed Universities respondents third preference was requires frequent up gradation of hardware and software. Least preference was indicated as making existing staff services redundant by State and Deemed University respondents and digital libraries cut down various personal or personalized services drastically by Central University respondents. Order of preference varies with type of university. The study was further extended to the category of user.

Table 4.82 Digital Environment Barriers Vs Category of User

S.No	Description	Research Scholars			Faculty Members			Total		
		Mean	Std.	Rank	Mean	Std.	Rank	Mean	Std.	Rank
1	More complex than the existing library system	2.65	.911	5	2.70	.903	5	2.67	.909	5
2	Needs training for the users to use digital library services	2.83	.861	3	2.81	.875	4	2.83	.865	4
3	Requires more investment on creation of digital libraries	2.93	.810	1	2.92	.825	2	2.93	.815	1
4	Requires frequent up gradation of hardware and software	2.90	.846	4	2.94	.882	1	2.91	.857	3
5	Non-existing of ownership of digital resources	2.93	.838	2	2.90	.805	3	2.92	.828	2
6	Making existing staff services redundant	2.05	1.138	8	2.04	1.129	7	2.04	1.135	8
7	Digital Libraries cut down various personal or personalized services drastically	2.09	1.125	7	2.03	1.083	8	2.07	1.112	7
8	Transactions will become machine to man rather than man to man	2.17	1.029	6	2.18	1.065	6	2.17	1.040	6

Table 4.82 indicates that opinion on digital environment barriers vary with the category of user. Research scholars have indicated Requires more investment on creation of digital libraries as first barrier followed by Non-existing of ownership of digital resources and Needs training for the users to use digital library services. Faculty members insisted on requires frequent up gradation of hardware and software followed by requires more investment on creation of digital libraries and Non-existing of ownership of digital resources. Least preference also interchange with research scholar and faculty members within Making existing staff services redundant and Digital Libraries cut down various personal or personalized services drastically. The study was further extended to the gender of the respondent.

Table 4.83 Digital Environment Barriers Vs Gender

S.No	Description	Male			Female			Total		
		Mean	Std.	Rank	Mean	Std.	Rank	Mean	Std.	Rank
1	More complex than the existing library system	2.67	.916	5	2.66	.892	5	2.67	.909	5
2	Needs training for the users to use digital library services	2.81	.864	4	2.87	.866	4	2.83	.865	4
3	Requires more investment on creation of digital libraries	2.92	.801	1	2.94	.844	2	2.93	.815	1
4	Requires frequent up gradation of hardware and software.	2.91	.868	3	2.92	.833	3	2.91	.857	3
5	Non-existing of ownership of digital resources.	2.91	.845	2	2.94	.788	1	2.92	.828	2
6	Making existing staff services redundant	2.03	1.122	8	2.08	1.162	8	2.04	1.135	8
7	Digital Libraries cut down various personal or personalized services drastically.	2.06	1.104	7	2.08	1.132	7	2.07	1.112	7
8	Transactions will become machine to man rather than man to man	2.16	1.038	6	2.19	1.044	6	2.17	1.040	6

Table 4.83 indicates that opinion on digital environment barriers vary with the gender of respondent. Male respondents have indicated that digital library requires more investment on creation of digital libraries as first barrier followed by non-existing of ownership of digital resources and requires frequent up gradation of hardware and software. Female respondents have insisted on non-existing of ownership of digital resources followed by requires more investment on creation of digital libraries and requires frequent up gradation of hardware and software. Least preference was indicated uniformly as making existing staff services redundant.

Table 4.84 Digital Environment Barriers – Overall Rank

S. No	Description	Overall	Central University	State University	Deemed University	Research Scholars	Faculty Members	Male	Female
1	More complex than the existing library system	5	4	4	5	5	5	5	5
2	Needs training for the users to use digital library services	4	1	5	2	3	4	4	4
3	Requires more investment on creation of digital libraries	1	3	1	1	1	2	1	2
4	Requires frequent up gradation of hardware and software	3	5	3	3	4	1	3	3
5	Non-existing of ownership of digital resources	2	2	2	4	2	3	2	1
6	Making existing staff services redundant	8	7	8	8	8	7	8	8
7	Digital Libraries cut down various personal or personalized services drastically	7	8	7	7	7	8	7	7
8	Transactions will become machine to man rather than man to man	6	6	6	6	6	6	6	6

Figure 4.26 Digital Environment Barriers – Overall Rank

Table 4.84 and Figure 4.26 shows that order of preference were somewhat uniform among the different categories of respondents and universities. Variables indicated were almost same but only the order changes.

Further hierarchical cluster test has also been administrated to identify the group of variables of digital environment barriers that are to be considered immediately. The dendrogram thus arrived has been shown in Figure 4.27.

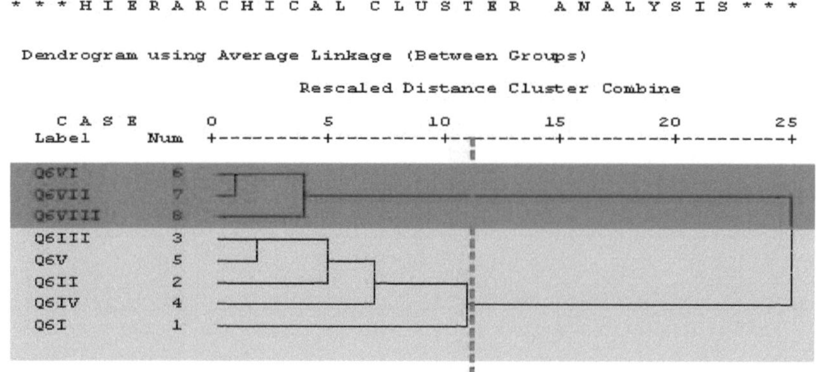

Figure 4.27 Digital Environment Barriers Cluster analyses

Figure 4.27 shows eight variables of digital environment barriers have cluster in to two groups. At 42% level, two clusters were formed. Cluster I comprises of three variables such as "Making existing staff services redundant"; "Digital Libraries cut down various personal or personalized services drastically and "Transactions will become machine to man rather than man to man". Cluster I can be named as ***"Professionals fear of change".*** Cluster II comprises of five variables such as "Requires more investment on creation of digital libraries", "Non-existing of ownership of digital resources", "Needs training for the users to use digital library services"; "Requires frequent up gradation of hardware and software" and "More complex than the existing library system". This cluster can be named as ***"Organizational fear of change".***

In order to identify the relation between variables, proximity analysis was administrated. The proximity matrix analysis will enable to identify the nearest and farthest variables. The proximity matrix has been employed for the digital environment barriers variables and the same is shown in Table 4.85.

Table 4.85 Digital Environment Barriers – Proximity Matrix

S. No	Description	1	2	3	4	5	6	7	8
1	More complex than the existing library system.	.000							
2	Needs training for the users to use digital library services.	3068.000	.000						
3	Requires more investment on creation of digital libraries.	3117.000	2143.000	.000					
4	Requires frequent up gradation of hardware and software.	2846.000	2874.000	2445.000	.000				
5	Non-existing of ownership of digital resources.	3075.000	2531.000	1982.000	2447.000	.000			
6	Making existing staff services redundant	4577.000	4891.000	5344.000	5033.000	4722.000	.000		
7	Digital Libraries cut down various personal or personalized services drastically.	4337.000	4813.000	5152.000	5021.000	5032.000	1856.000	.000	
8	Transactions will become machine to man rather than man to man	4052.000	4198.000	4379.000	4288.000	4547.000	2485.000	1981.000	.000

The proximity matrix Tables 4.85 enables to identify the closely associated variables and distinctly associated variables. The closely associated variables and distinctly associated variables are shown below.

Closely associated variables

- Transactions will become machine to man rather than man to man and Digital Libraries cut down various personal or personalized services drastically.
- Digital Libraries cut down various personal or personalized services drastically and Making existing staff services redundant.
- Non-existing of ownership of digital resources and Requires more investment on creation of digital libraries.

Distinctly associated variables

- "Making existing staff services redundant" and "Requires more investment on creation of digital libraries".
- "Digital Libraries cut down various personal or personalized services drastically" and "Requires more investment on creation of digital libraries".
- "Digital Libraries cut down various personal or personalized services drastically" and "Requires frequent up gradation of hardware and software".
- "Making existing staff services redundant" and "Requires frequent up gradation of hardware and software".
- "Digital Libraries cut down various personal or personalized services drastically" and "Non-existing of ownership of digital resources".

4.8 CONCLUSION

The analysis and interpretation of the data collected from the faculties and research scholars on the digital library management has been carried out and presented in this chapter. The findings and observation of the study and the suggestions have been highlighted in the next Chapter.

Chapter V

RESULTS & DISCUSSIONS

5.1 INTRODUCTION

In the previous chapter, detailed discussion on the analysis of data collected from the users in universities has been presented. The findings and observations are broadly classified based on results and discussions under appropriate headings with reference to the concerned tables and figures.

5.2 FINDINGS

The digital resource management was classified based on the concepts of Digital Knowledge Management as user expectation, essentiality, opinion and limitations. (Figure 4.3)

5.2.1 Sample

- A total of 2400 questionnaires were distributed to the faculty members and research scholars of 24 universities in Chennai. Out of which 2057 have respondent and the response rate works out to 85.71%. Demographic details of the respondents were presented according to the type of the university they belong to, gender, category of respondent etc.

5.2.2 Demographic Details

- Respondents population was more than 50% from deemed universities (58.5%), followed by state (32.1%) and central universities (9.3%). Respondents were classified in to two main categories namely Research scholars (70.1%) and Faculty members (29.9%). Gender wise classification indicates that male participants cater to 68.5% and female participants 31.5%. (Table 4.2 and Figure 4.2)

5.2.3 Digital Knowledge Management

- Variables were analyzed with different categories of respondents based on the type of university they belong to gender and category.

5.2.3.1 Visit to digital knowledge centre

- 61.3% of users visit digital knowledge resource centers daily which shows that users from all universities are dependent on the Digital Knowledge Resource Centers for their academic needs often.
- Male respondents were keen in visiting digital knowledge resource centers than female. This may be because male respondents were comparatively higher than female respondents in population.
- Research scholars were found utilizing more than faculty members as they are more in respondent population. Most of the respondents visit digital knowledge resource centers daily.

5.2.3.2 Working hours of the digital knowledge resource centers

- More than 77% of respondents have indicated that the working hours of digital knowledge resource centers was inconvenient to them for visiting.

- It can be suggested that the working hours can be made longer by utilizing the professional staff in shift basis with student volunteers.
- Invariably all the categories of respondents namely respondents from different types of universities, both gender and two categories have indicated that the current working timings was inconvenient except 5.3% of respondents from Central Universities.
- Central University digital knowledge resource centers were made available online with full time remote access and practically respondents need not depend on physical library working hours.

5.2.3.3 Convenient timings

- Convenient timings were categorized in to four sessions and two types of days namely working days and holidays.
- Most of the users prefer noon session for digital knowledge resource centers on both holidays and working days. But a few groups of respondents have indicated their convenience as late night session on holidays.
- Morning session was indicated as preference by respondents from Central universities.

5.2.4 Essentiality of Digital Knowledge Management

5.2.4.1 Digital resources

- Among 10 major publishers / suppliers of research output, IEEE online, ASCE and ACM were preferred more and Proquest was indicated at least preference. There exists uniformity among the respondents of categories and gender on digital resources.

5.2.4.2 Digital services

- Downloading of digital information from the internet was the top preferred digital service by 86.6% of respondents followed by e-literature search by 71.8% and e-newspaper by 68.6% of respondents.
- Downloading of digital information from the internet was indicated uniformly as top preference by respondents without gender bias and category.
- There exists variation in the order of preference among the respondents of different type of universities. E-literature search and e-newspapers were few among the top preferences indicated.

5.2.4.3 Digital user centric services

- Current Awareness Service (71.1%) was considered as the top preference followed by Epoxy servers (68.1%) and library automation (64.9%) by all respondents in general.
- Most of the choices and preferences were uniform among respondents of other categories and gender except respondents from central and deemed universities. Central university respondents insisted on library websites followed by Current Awareness Service and library automation.

5.2.4.4 Digital tools

- High speed internet access for getting information followed by Digital notice board and online book reservation and renewal system was the overall top preferences insisted.
- There exists lot of variation in order of preference among the respondents. Plasma TV was one among the least rated as the purpose of plasma TV is minimal in the context of application in library when compared to digital notice board or web OPAC etc.

- Male respondents and research scholars have indicated similar preferences whereas female respondents and faculty members indicate similar order of preference.

5.2.4.5 Digital service providers

- Except respondents from Deemed University all others have indicated federated search engine facilities (71.1%) as the first choice followed by networking facilities (67%) and SMS alert services (66.5%).
- On overall order of preference there exists variation depending on the category or gender or type of university the respondent belongs to still first and last preference of research scholars, faculties, male and female respondents were uniform.

5.2.4.6 Digital Service Policy

- Citation analysis and commercial reference management tools were the top preferences among most of the respondents and interchange in order with reference to the category or gender of the respondent.
- INFLIBNET Vidwan was the least preferred digital service policy which should be reconsidered and framed according to the need of the respondent or improve access facilities or the contents.

5.2.5 Dependence

- Dependence of Digital Knowledge Management is divided in to six major heads namely Digital Resources, Digital Services, Digital User Centric Services, Digital Tools, Digital Service Provides, Digital Service Policy.

5.2.5.1 Digital resources dependence

- IEEE online was depended more followed by ASME and Springer Link.
- Most of the publications of IEEE online covers higher education and professional education, where latest research output will be the vital need. Standard deviation was found to have minimum which indicates that there is no significant difference between the respondents.
- Except Central University respondents other categories have insisted IEEE online, followed by ASME and Springer Link and least dependence on Emerald publications.

5.2.5.2 Digital services dependence

- Among four scales with mean ranges between 3.99 and 2.83, which indicates that the respondents have indicated occasional to frequent usage.
- Downloading of information from the internet and digital repository services followed by e-newspaper and digital content management services were top ranked.
- E-abstracting and indexing services was least depended upon may be because the publisher themselves indexes their own publications.
- Male, female, research scholar and faculty members have indicated the order of preference uniformly. Opinion differs with the type of university.

5.2.5.3 Dependence on digital user centric services

- E-content management services were indicated as first preference followed by E-question bank services and library websites.

- Least preference was indicated as Current Awareness Service. Almost all the ranks vary with the different categories of respondents, except the least and third preference.

5.2.5.4 Dependence on digital tools

- To send e-mail to utilize the library services was the top preferred variable among the eight variables followed by printing and scanning facilities and high speed internet access facilities.
- Web OPAC was the least preference indicated. Gender wise and category wise ranking was similar among the respondents whereas the order of preference varied with the type of university they are affiliated to.

5.2.5.5 Dependence on digital service provides

- Networking facilities was the first preference followed by SMS alert service and open access knowledge resources material.
- Federated search engine facilities were the least preference indicated by all the respondents in general among nine different variables under dependence on digital service providers.
- Among category and gender wise analysis indicated that the order of preference was uniformly raked except the ranks indicated by the respondents from the type of university they are affiliated to.

5.2.5.6 Digital Service Policy Dependence

- Among 11 variables commercial reference management tools and services was indicated as the first preference followed by digital reference service and conference alert service.
- Least preference was indicated as Research gate uploading service. Except central and state type of university, respondents

from deemed, male and female, research scholar and faculty categories have indicated uniform ranking order with overall rank order.

5.2.6 Limitation

5.2.6.1 Limitation of Information

- 60% of respondents opinesthat the information available in web was contented to large extent, whereas 30% of respondents felt that the information has very little relevant content.
- Among three variables analyzed, only 50.1% of respondents felt that the digital libraries can provide better services than conventional library services from which it can be inferred that the conventional libraries can also provide equally better services as it has human touch with selective information which increases the relevancy.

5.2.6.2 Digital environment advantages

- Advantages of digital environment were analyzed with eight variables among which space management, anywhere and anytime access and easy retrieval was given more priority.
- Libraryservices shifted from 'just in case' to 'just in time' was indicated as the least preference from which it can be inferred that relevancy and accuracy was more important than time saving.Standard deviation was minimum among the responses which indicate that there was no significant difference between the opinions of the respondents.
- Except for the variable no maintenance all other variables were ranked uniformly among all the classification of respondents.
- Cluster analysis dendrogram provided three clusters for digital Environment advantages. ***Cluster I*** comprises of one variable ***"save more physical space".Cluster II*** comprises of one variable ***"Library services shifted from 'just in case' to 'just in time".***

Cluster I and ***Cluster II*** can be named together as ***Auxiliary digital policy.Cluster III*** comprises of six variables and this cluster can be named as ***Primary digital policy.***

- Proximity matrix test enabled to identify the closely associated variables.

- ***Closely associated variables were***

    - Networking of other libraries and enables networking of various internal resources
    - Enables networking of various internal resources and no maintenance
    - No maintenance and availability of information to all users simultaneously.

- ***Distinctly associated variables***

    - "Just in case and just in time" and "Save more Physical Space"
    - "Access from anywhere in any time" and "Just in case and just in time"
    - "Enables networking of various internal resources" and "save more physical space".
    - "Networking of other libraries" and "save more physical space".

5.2.6.3 Digital environment barriers

- Among eight variables requires more investment on creation of digital libraries was considered as the top barrier for setting up of digital environment followed by Non-existing of ownership of digital resources and requires frequent up gradation of hardware and software.
- Most of the variables require more skill for digital environment management and increased funds with respect to the advantages. Except the first and third preference, different classification of

respondents has indicated their ranks uniformly from which it can be inferred that more funds may be engaged for software, up gradation, skilled professionals, management, etc.

- Cluster analysis dendrogram provided three clusters for digital Environment advantages. ***Cluster I*** named as ***"Professionals fear of change"*** comprises of three variables. ***Cluster II*** comprises of five variables named as ***"Organizational fear of change".***
- Proximity matrix test enabled to identify the closely associated variables.

- ***Closely associated variables were***

    - Transactions will become machine to man rather than man to man and Digital Libraries cut down various personal or personalized services drastically.
    - Digital Libraries cut down various personal or personalized services drastically and Making existing staff services redundant.
    - Non-existing of ownership of digital resources and requires more investment on creation of digital libraries.

- ***Distinctly associated variables***

    - "Making existing staff services redundant" and "Requires more investment on creation of digital libraries".
    - "Digital Libraries cut down various personal or personalized services drastically" and "Requires more investment on creation of digital libraries".
    - "Digital Libraries cut down various personal or personalized services drastically" and "Requires frequent up gradation of hardware and software".
    - "Making existing staff services redundant" and requires frequent up gradation of hardware and software".

- "Digital Libraries cut down various personal or personalized services drastically" and "Non-existing of ownership of digital resources".

5.3 FINDINGS IN RELATION TO HYPOTHESES

The hypotheses stated in Chapter I, under section 1.6 which reads as-

1. There exist awareness on digital environment among the research scholars and faculties of the higher education institutions.
2. The users are well aware about the availability of various digital services in their institutions.
3. There exist awareness on various digital sources in their institutions among the users
4. The users are familiar in the use of ICT tools
5. There exist certain barriers in providing digital services and in acquiring of digital sources in the institutions have been proved in Chapter IV and found valid.

In the next chapter, based on the findings and observations, suggestions and recommendation have been formulated.

Chapter VI

SUMMARY & CONCLUSIONS

The Information and Communication Technology (ICT) and Library services are two faces of the same coin. The ICT internet and e-Governance have great potential in catering user needs in the present e-Knowledge Society. However, we have to be pragmatic in our approach in terms of electronic access to information. Availability, affordability, accessibility, acceptability and sustainability of the services should be kept in view in the application of ICT in the University Library and Information Centers. The summary and conclusion have been presented following aspects:

6.1 SUGGESTIONS

6.1.1 Digital Collection Development & ICT Applications

In view of the changing scenario in the Information

Communication Technology, it is suggested that the Knowledge

Managers shall strive for a right choice between printed and electronic media of publications.

6.1.2 Digital Knowledge Management and Online Database Services

In view of the significant contribution offered by e-mail services in the educational, research and development activities, it is suggested that the online database services such as IEEE online, ASME, ASCE, Springer Link, JCCC, IEBSCO, Emerald, Science direct, Proquest and E-Literature service, E-books services, E-abstracting/indexing, E-newspaper, Digital repository services, Digital Content Management services and downloading information from the internet shall be made available to the clientele of the libraries, as being provided by the libraries in the West.

6.1.3 Digital Knowledge Management & ICT Application Related Services

In view of the increased demand from the clientele of the libraries, it is suggested that the Digital Knowledge Management and ICT related application services such as the E-Content Management services, E-Question bank services, Library knowledge portal, remote access facility, automation, e-mail alerts services, Wi-Fi facility, Mobile alert services, online book reservation services, high speed internet access facility, Digital notice board, web OPAC should be provided to the clientele.

6.1.4 Knowledge Networking and E-Learning Services

Realising the importance of the knowledge networking and e-Learning Services, it is suggested that the University Librarian/ Knowledge Managers to go in for providing networking and e-Learning Services such as the Study material through web portal, National Knowledge Network (NKN), Spoken Tutorial IIT Bombay.

National Knowledge Network (NKN), Networking facilities of through DELNET, INDEST - AICTE, N-LIST,MANLIBNET, MALIBNET, ERNET, Spoken Tutorial IIT Bombay, Open Access Knowledge Resources Material (DOAJ, DOAB) Federated Search Engine Facilities, Social Network Services like FACEBOOK, LINKEDIN, TWITTER, WEB BLOG, WHATSUP towards the institutional development.

6.1.5 Digital Knowledge Management and Multimedia Literature Services

In view of the increasing demand and easy access on the multimedia applications, it is suggested that the e-librarian shall strive for the multimedia literature such as the Video Conference service and voice interactive, CD/DVD Materials, Video Courses (NPTEL), Web Courses, Online Educational Resources (OER) Learning like Couresera, MIT, Open courseware consortium in libraries.

6.1.6 Digital Knowledge Management and Research Supporting Services

Realising the significants of research supporting services, it is suggested that the services such as Citation analysis, Anti Plagiarism software service (Turnitin, Urkund), Content Management Software Service (Zoomla), Antivirus Software Service (Norton), Digital Copy rights Issue service, Google scholar uploading service, Research Gate uploading service, INFLIBNET Vidwan Uploading Service, IMPACT FACTOR and H – Index, Calculating service, Scholarly Communication of Information Services, Digital Conference Alert Services, Commercial Reference Management Tools and Services Learning Management Software (Moodle), Reference Management Software (ENDNOTE, REFERENCE MANAGER, REFWORKS, PAPERS) for Academic Research.

6.1.7 Reason for Poor Digital Knowledge Management Services

Realising the importance of the Digital Knowledge Management services in the library, it is suggested that the need for the ICT related education and hands on training to the information professionals and knowledge managers in the higher learning institutions for socio-economic and cultural development.

6.1.8 Strategies on Total Quality Management (TQM)

The concept of TQM is related to potential in all areas of libraries and much relevant in the present e-knowledge society. In view of this, it is suggested that the top management should motivate the LIS professionals to implement the TQM services towards the organizational development.

6.2 DIRECTIONS FOR FURTHER RESEARCH

Based on the study conducted, the researcher identified the following areas for further investigation:

- Use of digital resources among the library professionals in higher educational institutions.
- The study may be extended to specific domains such as engineering, science and technology and medical related fields towards the Job satisfaction among the library professionals.
- The study can be extended to public libraries and special libraries about the job satisfactions.
- The comparative study is in need for faculty in regional, state, national and international levels in relation to job satisfaction in LIS professionals.

The study may be extended also to library professionals working in corporate libraries in view of the job satisfaction.

6.3 CONCLUDING REMARKS

From the overall analysis an order of preference was uniform among male, female, research scholar and faculty members. Digital environment, resources, usage and dependence solely depends on the initiatives of the individual and the policies of the institutions. Users should be educated and motivated to fade down the barriers on digital environment. Combination of digital environment with conventional services may give more relevant and accurate usable information. Users are aware of latest technologies and resources but professionals can help them to reach out more relevant information with the strategies and technological dependences.

From the foregoing chapters, it is clear that the application of ICT in the University Library and Information Centers in and around Chennai (Madras) is in a slow pace, which affected the implementation of ICT in various sections of the library. This consequently affected the provisions of ICT based services and products. This state of affairs has been largely due to inadequate finances and lack of motivation etc. The study presents the current state-of-the-art of libraries and information centers considered for the survey.

The analysis of the survey brings forth the positive attitude of the library staff towards ICT applications. Further, the survey identifies the various reasons that come in the way of implementing ICT in a most comprehensive manner. It is the need of the hour that authorities concerned should realize this current situation and take immediate and appropriate steps in this regard. It is in this context, the suggestions and recommendations of the study would be relevant and useful. The Digital Knowledge Management and ICT application tools are the emerging concept in the present digital knowledge era in the developing countries like India. The application of ICT is a novel phenomenon in Indian library context and that novelty will give way to recessions that demand will be driven by competition among librarian and by the prospects of improving work culture in library and information centers.

ABSTRACT

Digital Knowledge Management (DKM) plays a vital role in the present digital knowledge Era. It provides effective, efficient information and knowledge management services to the library user community in time and on demand. Knowledge management represented as a cross-disciplinary domain which can relate to a wide range of disciplines and technologies such as cognitive science, knowledge based management system, Library and information science, Documentation management, Relational and object orientated database and management of information and people. The Digital Knowledge Management as a tool for supporting the creation, achieving and sharing of valued information to facilitate the web based solution to know-how the technologies on Digital /Electronics learning to support the ICT Technologies towards organizational development.

The Information and Communication Technology tools are inevitable for **K**nowledge **A**ccess and **S**haring **I**nformation for **R**esources **A**pproach **O**bjectives (KASIRAO) in the present e-knowledge society. The ICT serves as a tool for efficient Management of Information, that is storage, retrieval, processing communication, diffusing and sharing of knowledge for Socio-Economic and Cultural Development. The impact of Information Communication Technology (ICT) encourages the library user community to search and to retrieve the required information. It also helps the knowledge economy by promoting Digital Knowledge Management and objectively that the application of Information Communication Technology in the University Library and Information Centers would certainly put on order and bring out a sequence operations in Library and Information Management Environment (LISME) without much of human interventions.

Based on the conceptual analysis view, the research study identifies the State-of-the-Art of the Digital Knowledge Management and ICT applications in the State, Central and Deemed University Libraries in Chennai. The study identifies the factors like lack of finance and training to hinder the promotion of ICT in Libraries and to promote it offers suggestions for effective implementation of ICT application tools for digital knowledge management services in the Library and Information Centers.